The Escape Boat

Mastering the Art of Timely Decisions in an Unpredictable Workplace

Anilesh Mukherjee & Om Sharma

Qurate
quratebooks.com

The Escape Boat

The Escape Boat
Anilesh Mukherjee & Om Sharma

Published in 2025

© Published by

Qurate Books Pvt. Ltd.
Goa 403523, India
www.quratebooks.com
Tel: 1800-210-6527, Email: info@quratebooks.com

ISBN: 978-93-5898-542-9

DEDICATION

To those who choose courage over comfort and lead not with authority, but with authenticity.

To the curious minds, quiet doers, and silent warriors who rise when it's easier to retreat.

And to our families, your unwavering belief has been the wind beneath every word.

A Note from the Authors

This book is more than a manuscript; it is a reflection of our journey, filled with lessons born from lived experiences, tested ideas, and heartfelt intent.

The Escape Boat isn't just a metaphor; it's a mirror for anyone navigating moments of uncertainty, transition, or reinvention.

We dedicate this work to everyone who has ever felt stuck but refused to stay that way.

May our stories, learnings, and experiments become the compass you didn't know you needed.

This isn't just a book, it's your lifeline. Hold on tight!

Anilesh Mukherjee & Om Sharma

PREFACE

The Courage to Row When You're Stuck

Have you ever felt like you're going through the motions, working hard, showing up, checking all the boxes, yet deep inside, something feels off?

You're not burned out exactly. You're not ungrateful. But you feel stuck, disconnected and maybe even invisible.

Do you think it is a failure? No, it is not; it is your inner voice nudging you.

We wrote this book for this moment. Let us try to demystify this situation.

Review the scene below:

A Common Scene, A Quiet Struggle

Picture this: You're in a meeting where everything looks polished, people nod, dashboards shine, and targets are ticked. But inside, you're wondering, "Why am I still not fulfilled?"

We've sat with professionals at every level, from freshers to CXOs, who've whispered the same words:

"I don't feel like myself anymore."

We've seen star performers become silent passengers. Teams lose their edge. Brilliant minds caught in repetitive tasks, waiting for a 'better time' to pivot. These aren't rare cases; they're real, frequent, and quietly growing.

Why This Book Isn't Another 'Fix You' Manual

This book won't tell you to chase promotions, hustle harder, or reinvent your LinkedIn profile. It's not a quick fix or motivational jargon.

Instead, it offers 3Ps that are something much deeper: Perspective, Permission, and Power.

It's about creating your own mental and emotional Escape Boat, not to run away, but to stay afloat when the world around you shakes.

Not because you're weak. But because you're wise enough to know when systems break, it's time to build your own support.

Why We Say "Escape"

Escape here doesn't mean quitting or giving up.

It means stepping out of toxic patterns. Saying no to misaligned roles. Breaking free from the need to 'keep up' when the direction doesn't feel right anymore.

"Escape isn't about running away; it's about rising above, choosing clarity over chaos, courage over comfort, and your true self over the noise."
- Anilesh Mukherjee

Why a "Boat"?

Life and work don't always sail smoothly. There are storms, layoffs, sudden role changes, shifting cultures, pressure to adapt overnight, and to deliver perfection with fewer resources. And somewhere in this chase, we start to burn out silently.

A boat is not built for luxury; it is built to survive. It is your personal space of purpose, light enough to stay afloat, focused enough to keep moving. While the world feels like it's drowning in noise, this is your space to breathe, reflect, and move forward with clarity.

Sometimes, staying afloat isn't weakness; it's wisdom.
The Escape Boat is your reminder!

How will you handle this situation?

There are the Six Layers of Escape.

Before we build the boat, we need to understand what is anchoring us to get stuck in a situation. Is it across stories, reflections, and patterns?

These are the six invisible layers that often trap us:

1. Fear of Judgment – "What will people think if I step out or slow down?"
2. Fear of Rejection – "What if I speak up and they stop including me?"
3. Impostor Syndrome – "I'm not really as good as they think. I better not mess up."
4. Scarcity Mindset – "What if this is the best I'll ever get?"
5. Toxic Comparison – "They're doing better. Maybe I'm not enough."
6. Learned Helplessness – "I've tried changing things before. Nothing works."

Each of these layers becomes an excuse dressed up as logic. They sound reasonable, but they quietly stop us from growing.

Most often, we have our own ways to say 'No'; however, excuses always come to our mind. Do you resonate or reciprocate with the feelings?

The Excuses We All Know Too Well

- "Now isn't the right time"
- "Maybe next quarter"

- "Let's not rock the boat"
- "I should just be grateful I have a job"
- "It's not that bad"
- "I'll wait for my manager to notice"
- "Whom should I reach out to?"

Don't waste energy fighting your excuses, face the fears and doubts holding you back. Focus on growth, and let the right mindset guide you through.

Why We Wrote This Book?

When we were moving from Individual Contributor to a Leadership role (leader of leaders), we encompassed so much of learnings from our superiors, which made us stand taller as we are today.

The biggest breakthroughs do not come from grand strategies; they come from small moments of truth.

This book is a collection of those moments from our experience(s) and experiment(s), and what we have learnt from the personas we have met in our lives. We learned 3R's – Reflect, Reset and Rise.

This book intends to make individuals with different roles you hold in your current capacity.

Who should read?

- Corporate Leaders who want to make a change and are silently observing
- Mid Managers who want to hustle (questioning the status quo)
- All the change agents, coaches, creators, and anyone craving realignment with their deeper purpose
- Thought Leaders (new), Thinkers, Professors, Students,

Entrepreneurs and Professionals who feel stuck despite 'doing everything right'

If you've ever wondered:

- "Why am I feeling lost, even when I'm doing well?"
- "What if there's another way to succeed, without losing myself?"
- "Can I be strong and sensitive in the corporate world?"

Then this is your invitation.

Let's Get Real, Let's Get Going

You don't need to escape the world. But you do need to escape the version of yourself that no longer fits.

Build the boat. Row when needed. Anchor when tired. Reflect often. And most importantly, stay human, always.

"The Escape Boat doesn't take you away from life.
It brings you back to who you were before the world told you who to be."

Welcome Aboard!

With Empathy,

Om Sharma & Anilesh Mukherjee

Story Teller | Author | Researcher | Transformation Coach | People First Leader

ACKNOWLEDGMENTS

Co-authoring this book has been a deeply enriching journey, both personally and professionally. As we navigated ideas, debates, and discoveries, one thing remained constant: our shared commitment to offering insights that empower, challenge, and transform.

We're deeply grateful to the mentors, thinkers, and change-makers whose wisdom has influenced the ideas within these pages. To the clients, colleagues, and teams we've worked with, you brought these lessons to life with your courage, challenges, and breakthroughs.

A heartfelt thank you to our families, whose unwavering support and understanding carried us through this creative endeavor. Your belief in us is our strength.

To every reader holding this book in hand, thank you for trusting us to walk beside you on your journey. May this be more than a book; may it be a spark that fuels your transformation.

Finally, to our parents, siblings, partner, children, friends, and professional guides, thank you for your presence in our lives. You've shaped who we are, and we hold deep gratitude for your constant encouragement, love, and wisdom.

TABLE OF CONTENTS

The Escape Boat: Why We Drift from Opportunities and How to Row Back to Purpose

SECTION V – SUSTAIN & SCALE

SECTION I –

THE INVISIBLE STRUGGLE

1 WELCOME ABOARD TO THE ESCAPE BOAT

Is this Me?

What's the one thing I keep postponing, and what's the story I tell myself and others about why?

- Am I calling it "bad timing," or is it actually just fear of discomfort disguised as logic?
- Do I wait for 'perfect conditions,' or do I create momentum with what I have?
- Am I scared someone will outshine me, or am I just afraid of being seen?
- When opportunity knocked last time, did I open the door-or pretend not to hear it?

Imagine standing on the shore, gazing at a vast ocean of opportunities. Somewhere on the horizon lies your chance to transform your life, but instead of diving in, you find yourself boarding a metaphorical "The Escape Boat." This boat, constructed from excuses and fears, serves as a refuge from the uncertainty and risks that come with seizing opportunities. It feels safe, familiar, and reassuring, but it also keeps you anchored in place, far from progress.

Based on a series of informal interviews and pulsecheck surveys conducted with professionals across ITeS, GCC (Captive centres), healthcare workers, educators, students, corporate executives, and startup founders, a familiar pattern of internal dialogues emerged. These statements reflect a psychological safety net, what we call "**The Escape Boat**"; where excuses often disguise hesitation, fear, or comfort with the status quo.

The Escape Boat: Real Excuses from Real People

In our conversations across industries and walks of life, we heard a variety of "*safe*" statements, repeated so often that they almost seem like universal truths. But when we listened closely, we realized they weren't truths at all. They were gentle ways people convinced themselves not to act, not to risk, not to grow.

Here are some of the most common phrases professionals and students alike shared with us:

- "Let me think about it... later"

  Our Interpretation: I'm afraid to decide because I might be wrong.

- "What if I fail in front of everyone?"

  Our Interpretation: I don't want to lose face or be seen as incompetent.

- "This isn't how we usually do things"

  Our Interpretation: I'm uncomfortable breaking tradition, even if it's broken.

- "I'll start once things settle down"

  Our Interpretation: I'm waiting for a 'perfect' time that may never come.

- "Someone else is already doing it better"

  Our Interpretation: I've already talked myself out of trying.

- "What if they judge me for trying?"

  Our Interpretation: I fear criticism more than I desire change.

- "Maybe next month... or next year."

  Our Interpretation: I want the outcome, but I'm avoiding the effort.

- "It's safer to stay in my zone."
  Our Interpretation: Growth sounds good, but safety feels better.
- "I'll wait for the perfect moment."
  Our Interpretation: Procrastination disguised as preparation.
- "Why should I change if no one else is?"
  Our Interpretation: I want permission from others to move forward.

The Escape Boat is not inherently evil; it is a product of human psychology. It represents our instinctive desire to avoid discomfort, failure, or judgment. Yet, by choosing this vessel of retreat over the uncharted waters of opportunity, we limit our growth and potential. The excuses that form this boat:

"I am too young or new in my job"

"I'm too old to start something new"

"I don't have the right network or contacts"

"What if my idea isn't good enough?"

"They won't listen to someone like me"

"I'm just not a risk-taker"

"My job is stable; I shouldn't rock the boat"

"There's no use trying if the system won't change"

"Let the younger generation do this"

"I don't have the time or energy anymore"

"Right now, my kids are small, school routines are hectic, and there's no one else to manage things; maybe once they grow up, I'll finally have time for myself"

These are not justifications for inaction but barriers to self-discovery and success.

Understanding why we board this boat is crucial. It's not simply about laziness or lack of ambition. The Escape Boat is often a response to deeply ingrained fears: fear of failure, fear of judgment, and fear of stepping outside our comfort zones. These fears are natural, but must be confronted if we are to break free from this cycle of retreat.

These are not just statements. They are mental habits, emotional reactions, and psychological safety nets that keep people from taking action.

This book aims to help you recognize your own The Escape Boat, and more importantly, learn how to step out of it and swim toward the life you were meant to build.

Why Opportunities Feel So Hard to Catch

Sometimes, opportunities feel like they're always just out of reach. They don't show up looking easy or obvious; they often come wrapped in risk, discomfort, or tough decisions. That's what makes them tricky. Let's break down why:

1. Opportunities Don't Wait Around

Opportunities are like shooting stars; they show up quickly, and if you don't act fast, they're gone. They don't come with loud announcements or flashing signs. Most of the time, we have to spot them, decide quickly, and take a leap. That's hard for many of us, especially when fear kicks in.

2. They Don't Come with Guarantees

Let's face it; no opportunity comes with a 100% success guarantee. There's always some doubt. For example, someone might see their dream job posted online, but instead of applying, they tell themselves, "I'm probably not good enough," or "What if I fail?" That fear of "what if" stops them from even trying.

3. Our Minds Hold Us Back

Our brains naturally prefer comfort. It's safer to stay where we are, doing what we already know. So, when something new shows up; even if it could be amazing, our mind highlights the risks instead of the rewards. We focus on what could go wrong more than what could go right.

4. Society Teaches Us to Play Safe

From a young age, many of us hear things like "Don't take risks" or "Be practical." Messages like these can quietly shape our behavior. So even when we do want to take a chance, a voice in our head says, "What will people think?" or "That's not for someone like you."

The Real Problem: It's Not the Opportunity; It's the Way, We See It

Opportunities aren't really that rare. What is rare is the mindset to recognize and act on them. Most of the time, it's our 'own' fear, hesitation, and past experiences that create the feeling of "missed chances." But once we become aware of these mental blocks, we can start shifting our approach, and stop watching those shooting stars disappear.

The Escape Boat: A Metaphor for Our Excuses

The idea of The Escape Boat is a way to compare how we handle life using the example of a boat. It shows how we often use excuses to avoid moving forward.

Think of your life like a sailboat. To move in the right direction, you need a steering wheel (which is like your values) and a destination (your goals). In the same way, you need the right mindset to face life's challenges.

But sometimes, fears are like holes in the boat. Instead of fixing these fears properly, many people just cover them up with excuses, which keeps them stuck instead of moving ahead.

This mindset is fueled by:

- **We Like Being Comfortable:** Most of us love routines. We prefer staying where we feel safe, even if it means missing out on something better. Trying new things often means stepping into the unknown, and that feels scary

- **Excuses Feel Safer than Risks:** Phrases like *"I'm not ready"*, *"This isn't the right time"*, or *"What if I fail?"* sound logical, but they're just anchors. They hold us back while life keeps moving

- **We Overthink Too Much:** Ever thought about doing something exciting but then spent so much time thinking about the risks that you ended up doing nothing? That's overthinking. And it often comes from fear, fear of failing, being judged, or not being perfect

- **We Care Too Much About What Others Think:** Culture, society, or even family expectations can quietly push us to play safe. If everyone around you avoids risks, it's hard to be the one who takes the leap. So, we follow the crowd, and miss our path

Getting Out of The Escape Boat

The "safe" boat made of excuses may keep you dry for a while, but it won't get you anywhere. You'll just float. The real magic happens when you step out, even if it means getting a little wet.

Sure, the waters of opportunity are uncertain, but they're full of growth, learning, success, and self-respect.

Think About This...

Are you waiting for the perfect time?

Are you telling yourself "Maybe later" too often?

Are your doubts louder than your dreams?

If the answer is yes, then maybe... just maybe... you're on The Escape Boat.

The journey to growth starts the moment you stop saying "What if I fail?" and start saying "What if this works?"

Will you let your excuses steer the boat, or will you finally take the wheel and head toward something better?

The choice is yours!

2 SHOOTING STARS AND MISSED CHANCES

We've all seen a shooting star, just a quick flash across the night sky. It's beautiful, unexpected, and gone before you know it. Life throws us similar moments, chances that shine brightly for a short time, and if we don't act fast, they slip away.

Opportunities often don't come with warning signs or second chances. They show up quietly, and if we spend too much time thinking, doubting, or waiting for the "right time," we miss them.

Take Martha's story, for example. She worked as a smart and trusted team leader in a large IT company. One day, she was offered a 6-month assignment in Singapore to lead a big project. It wasn't permanent, just a trial, but with huge potential.

Instead of grabbing it, Martha got stuck in her own head:

"What if I fail?"

"What if they don't keep me on?"

"What will people say if I return early?"

So, she said no.

A junior teammate, who was less experienced but more open to taking a chance, said yes right away. That teammate led the project well, impressed leadership, and got promoted with a permanent role abroad.

Martha stayed where she was safe, but full of "what ifs."

And she's not alone. According to Psychology Today, nearly 73% of professionals admit they regret not saying yes to a major opportunity because of fear, self-doubt, or just overthinking.

A moment to reflect:

- How many shooting stars have passed you by because you were too afraid to jump?
- How many times did you say, “Maybe later”… and later never came?

Opportunities don’t always knock twice. The question is: will you wait and watch, or will you move and catch them while they’re within reach?

The Psychology of Hesitation

Hesitation is often born from the interplay of fear, self-doubt, and overthinking. When an opportunity presents itself, the mind becomes a battleground for conflicting thoughts: "What if I am unsuccessful?" "Am I ready for this?" "Is this the right choice?"

Hesitation is not just a pause; it’s a mental and emotional response driven by fear, self-doubt, perfectionism, and risk aversion.

The brain is designed to protect us. It sees any uncertainty as a potential threat. When an opportunity presents itself, especially if it's outside our comfort zone, our brain doesn't say "Go for it!"; it says, “Hold on. Is this safe?”

Consider Peter, a mid-level operations manager in a logistics firm. When his company began a new digital transformation wing, he was invited to lead the pilot automation program. Peter had no formal training in tech, and despite his interest, he replied, “I think someone from IT is better suited.” The role went to a consultant who had less knowledge of the business but more belief in themselves. Within two years, Peter was reporting to that same consultant.

Key mental blocks like these often shape hesitation:

- Impostor Syndrome: "I'm not qualified enough"
- Fear of Judgment: "What if I fail in public?"
- Overthinking Bias: "Let me think this through 20 more times"
- Loss Aversion: "I might lose what I already have"

Hesitation comes from an overactive risk calculator in the brain. It weighs losses heavier than gains;even if those gains could be life-changing.

The Fear of Failure

Consider the story of Thomas, a talented painter living in a small town. For years, he poured his heart into his art, dreaming of exhibiting his work in galleries across the country. One day, a renowned art curator visited his town and offered Thomas an opportunity to showcase his paintings in a prestigious gallery in the city. But he hesitated, plagued by the fear of rejection and criticism. He worried that he wasn't good enough, that his work wouldn't be well-received.

While the opportunity was rare and promising, his hesitation caused him to decline. Months later, he regretted his decision as he watched lesser-known artists thrive in the same gallery. His story serves as a poignant reminder that the fear of failure often magnifies risks and obscures possibilities.

The Paralysis of Overthinking

Another psychological barrier is the tendency to overanalyse. Take the example of Steve, an ambitious young professional. He was offered a leadership role in his company; a chance to lead a team and influence strategic decisions. Instead of accepting the offer outright, Steve spent weeks analyzing the pros and cons. He agonized over whether he was ready, whether the team would respect him, and whether he could juggle the added responsibilities.

By the time Steve made up his mind to accept, the opportunity had passed, and the position was given to someone else. His story highlights how overthinking can lead to "analysis paralysis," robbing us of the chance to act.

The Role of Self-Doubt

Self-doubt is often the silent thief that steals opportunities. Many hesitate not because the opportunity is unworthy, but because they underestimate their ability to rise to the occasion. This mindset keeps us anchored in hesitation, preventing us from exploring the unknown.

Example:

The Trampoline Truth: What We Teach Kids but Forget as Adults

Remember jumping on a trampoline as a kid? Every fall wasn't a failure; it was part of the fun. You bounced back. The harder you fell, the higher you jumped next. That's what made it exciting.

Now think about this: when a child falls on a trampoline, we cheer them on; "Get up! Try again! You've got this!" We expect them to bounce back.

But somewhere along the way at work, in relationships, in life, we stop doing that for ourselves. We fall and stay down. We worry about how it looks, what others think, and whether we'll ever get back up.

Just like trampolines, life will push you down sometimes, but it also gives you the power to bounce back.

In fact, in many cultures, there's a belief:

"There is always an 11th hour or an 11th day",

A last-minute chance, a fresh start, a new opening. Whether it's a lost deal, a failed exam, or a rejected job application; it's not the end unless you stop trying.

In Japan, they call it Kaizen, Continuous Improvement.

In the U.S., it's Resilience.

In India, it's Jugaad or Workaround, the ability to adapt and find a way forward.

Different names. Same spirit. Bounce back. Don't break down.

If you'd clap for a child who got back up on the trampoline, why not clap for yourself when life knocks you down?

Opportunity Windows: Why They're So Brief

Opportunities are like open windows during a storm; they don't stay open for long.

Timing is one of the most underestimated variables in life. You could be the most talented person in the room, but if you don't act when the door opens, someone else will walk through it.

When someone asked me how long an opportunity lasts, I replied, just as long as a biscuit stays intact when dipped in tea.

"An opportunity is like a biscuit in hot tea; wait too long, and it crumbles away"

Example: Consider Microsoft's offer to Yahoo in 2008. Yahoo was struggling, but had a loyal user base. Microsoft offered $44 billion to acquire them. Yahoo hesitated, thinking the offer undervalued their worth. They rejected it. In the following years, Yahoo's value plummeted. By 2017, they were sold to Verizon for just $4.5 billion; a fraction of what was offered.

In human psychology, this is referred to as the "window of readiness". Every decision has an optimal moment. Beyond that timeframe, the effort needed, both emotionally and mentally, to initiate action rises significantly.

A Harvard Business Review article describes this as the "Motivation-Action Gap": The longer you wait, the more reasons your brain creates not to act.

Opportunities are inherently transient, often appearing at the confluence of timing, circumstance, and action. Their brevity is dictated by several factors:

1. The Pace of Change

The modern world moves at an unprecedented speed. Consider the story of Arjun, an entrepreneur who had an idea for a mobile app that could streamline grocery shopping. He shared his concept with friends but delayed acting on it, thinking he had ample time to refine the idea. Months later, he discovered that another company had launched a similar app, rendering his concept obsolete.

The rapid pace of change in technology, markets, and trends means that opportunities are fleeting. Waiting too long can result in missed chances.

2. Competitive Dynamics

Opportunities are rarely exclusive; they are often visible to multiple people at once. A compelling real-life example comes from the corporate world.

Example: In a school, the teacher announced that a new class captain was needed to lead an upcoming inter-school event. It was a chance to represent the class, work closely with teachers, and build leadership skills.

A few students raised their hands right away, excited and ready, even if they weren't sure of every detail.

But others stayed quiet.

- Some thought, "What if I mess it up?"
- Some said, "Let me think about it. Maybe I'll say yes tomorrow."
- Others waited to see who else would step forward.

By the time they made up their minds, the teacher had already chosen one of the first volunteers, someone who took the chance with confidence, not certainty.

That student went on to represent the class, learned new skills, made new friends, and even got recognized in the school assembly.

The competitive nature of many opportunities means that hesitation can lead to losing out, as others with quicker reflexes seize the moment.

3. Circumstantial Shifts

Opportunities come and go as situations change fast. Consider the story of Meera, a journalist who was offered an exclusive interview with a high-profile figure. The interview was time-sensitive, dependent on the availability of the guest. Meera hesitated, wanting more time to prepare. In the interim, the guest's schedule changed, and the opportunity vanished.

This example underscores the reality that opportunities often rely on specific conditions, and these conditions can shift unexpectedly.

Real-Life Parallel: A Missed Bus vs. A Life Opportunity

Shooting stars, much like opportunities, remind us to act swiftly, decisively, and with courage. They teach us to embrace imperfection, overcome hesitation, and recognize the fleeting nature of life's chances. The above stories illustrate the profound impact that hesitation and the brevity of opportunity windows can have on our journey.

Ultimately, the question is: Will you let hesitation dim your light, or will you take a bold leap to reach for the stars? Opportunities are no different. They rarely wait. They are usually meant for those ready to act, not those still building courage.

The choice is yours, and the time is now!

3 INSIDE THE CORPORATE WHIRLPOOL: THE PSYCHOLOGY OF THE ESCAPE BOAT AND UNETHICAL CORPORATE BEHAVIOUR

Rita prepared for months to present her innovative idea at a company-wide meeting. But just before her turn, self-doubt crept in: "What if they don't like it? What if I mess up?" She quietly backed out, letting someone else take the spotlight.

A month later, that very idea, pitched by someone else, won the department an innovation award.

"It's not always the setback that holds us back, it's the seatbelt we strap ourselves into before even starting."

Let's face it, corporate life can feel like a spinning washing machine. One moment you're working toward your goals, and the next, you're caught between what your heart says, what your company expects, and how fast you want to grow. It's easy to get confused or overwhelmed.

In the middle of all this, people often start taking what we call "The Escape Boat." It's not a real boat, but a mental habit. It's the part of us that avoids taking action, dodges tough conversations, stays quiet when something feels wrong, or delays stepping into new ideas. We tell ourselves it's the "safe" thing to do. But deep down, it usually comes from fear; fear of failure, fear of being judged, or fear of rocking the boat.

And it's not just one or two people doing this. Many companies unintentionally create work cultures where it feels better to "play it safe" than to speak up or try something new. People are often rewarded more for fitting in than for thinking differently. Over time, this creates teams full of quiet observers instead of active doers.

Think about how many smart, talented people you know who are stuck in roles they've outgrown, not because they can't do more, but because they're afraid to take a risk. Maybe they once had an idea, but someone laughed it off. Or maybe they saw something unethical but stayed quiet because they were afraid of the consequences.

These aren't just personal choices; they're shaped by how workplaces operate. When the system encourages staying silent or choosing comfort over courage, it's no wonder people "float" instead of moving forward.

This book is here to help you see those patterns clearly. Through real stories, coaching experiences, and solid research, we'll explore why people take The Escape Boat, how it affects careers and culture, and most importantly, what you can do to step out of it. It's not about blame; it's about taking back control of your work life and doing it with integrity and purpose.

Whether you're sitting in the boardroom or a shared desk space, this tendency is real, and it's holding back not just individuals but entire organizations. But with the right mindset, you can row your own boat and set a better course.

The Ethical Blind Spot in Tech Teams – A Case of the "Silent Algorithm"

A global technology firm launched a machine learning-driven recruitment tool designed to streamline candidate shortlisting. The algorithm was trained on historical hiring data, touted as "unbiased" and "efficient." Within weeks, however, internal whispers surfaced: the tool was consistently ranking female candidates lower for leadership roles.

Rather than raise immediate concerns, many within the data science and product teams chose to "float", a psychological response that aligns with what we term The Escape Boat.

Engineers rationalized it was an "issue of data, not design." Product owners avoided conversations fearing it would derail timelines. HR stakeholders stayed quiet, citing a lack of technical expertise.

The Psychology Behind the Drift:

As Kate O'Neill suggests in *Tech Humanist*, technology must serve humanity's best interests, not just scale efficiencies. But when humans behind technology disengage due to fear, deadlines, or hierarchical pressures, ethics become an afterthought.

> "Technology reflects the values of its creators, and when those creators fear speaking up, the values get distorted."
>
> *Kate O'Neill, Tech Humanist*

This situation exemplifies systemic The Escape Boat behavior:

1. Dodging Innovation: Data scientists hesitated to challenge the training model, fearing backlash or additional workload.

2. Evading Accountability: Product owners reframed ethical concerns as "edge cases," preferring to release on schedule than to re-engineer.

3. Rationalizing Unethical Choices: Leadership dismissed the findings, labeling them as "not statistically significant."

Eventually, a whistleblower raised the issue externally, resulting in reputational damage, legal scrutiny, and public outcry. The company retracted the tool, issued a public apology, and implemented an AI Ethics Committee; too late to undo the damage.

The Cost of Silent Disengagement in Tech

When fear overrides ethics and when internal culture rewards silence over scrutiny, innovation becomes tainted. The Escape

Boat mindset, in tech particularly, doesn't just risk individual integrity, it can code bias into systems that scale across millions of lives.

What Could Have Helped?

- Emotional Literacy Workshops (for teams to process fear and risk in innovation)
- Ethics-First Sprint Reviews (as checkpoints before major releases)
- Bias Audits & Red Teams to interrogate algorithmic integrity

As *Kate O'Neill* wisely says, "The future of humanity is increasingly shaped by how we design our technologies."

So, ask yourself:

Am I floating or leading?

Because in the tech world, your silence can ship as code!

The Escape Boat Psychology at Work: Why Saying "No" Feels So Hard

Have you ever found yourself saying "yes" at work just because you didn't want to upset someone, even when you were already overloaded? You're not alone. In many workplaces, people find it really hard to say "no," even when they know they should. And it's not just about manners; it's about deep, invisible pressures we all feel.

As William Meller, a writer and a professional, shares in his research, many working professionals go through an inner battle. They don't want to disappoint their manager, let down teammates, or break the silent rules of "always being helpful." This pressure often comes from our own need to be liked, to be seen as cooperative, or just to avoid conflict. So, we end up taking on more than we can handle.

This people-pleasing mindset, though often well-intentioned, can slowly wear us down. Workplaces that constantly praise "team players" without clear boundaries can accidentally create a culture where no one feels safe to decline extra tasks. Over time, people begin to say "yes" even when they're running on empty.

This leads to what experts call "role overload", when someone is juggling so many things that they start dropping the ball. And when that happens, some start cutting corners or making poor choices just to keep up. That's where The Escape Boat mindset kicks in: doing the bare minimum, avoiding new responsibilities, or disengaging quietly because it feels safer than speaking up.

Example: Peter, a senior analyst in a finance company, was known for always saying "yes" to extra work. He didn't want his boss to think he was lazy or non-cooperative. But soon, he was drowning in deadlines. Instead of asking for help, he started copying old reports and reusing content just to meet timelines. In trying too hard to please everyone, he overlooked the quality of his work, and it cost him a warning letter.

Example: The Resistant Operations Manager

When the Project Manager proposed adopting an AI-based scheduling tool to optimize workforce planning and reduce manual errors, the Operations Manager immediately pushed back.

"*We're already stretched thin. My team can't handle learning a new system right now. Besides, we've been doing this manually for years; it's not broken.*"

Despite evidence showing the tool could save over 20 hours a week and reduce scheduling conflicts by 40%, the Operations Manager cited overcommitment and lack of bandwidth as barriers. Ironically, this refusal led to more inefficiencies, increased errors, and team burnout, forcing junior staff to cut corners to meet performance metrics.

This classic case of “role overload” meets resistance to change, where a rigid mindset and fear of disrupting existing workflows override the long-term benefits of innovation, ultimately reinforcing an unsustainable, ethically vulnerable culture.

“Are you working to grow, or to just work?”

Sometimes, we board The Escape Boat not because we’re lazy, but because we’ve forgotten how to say "no" and still feel worthy.

Unethical Corporate Behavior: From Boardrooms to Cubicles

Understanding Ethical Missteps in the Workplace

In the corporate world, challenges related to ethics can arise at any level, from top executives to entry-level employees. These challenges often stem from decisions that prioritize short-term gains over long-term integrity.

Lessons from Notable Corporate Missteps

1. Leadership Decisions and Their Impact

High-profile cases like ‘Enron’ and ‘Satyam’ have shown how decisions at the top can have far-reaching consequences. Enron's complex financial maneuvers and Satyam's falsified accounts led to significant financial losses and eroded public trust.

2. The Importance of Data Security

The 'Marriott' data breach, affecting over 334 million customers, highlighted the critical need for robust cybersecurity measures. Inadequate security practices can lead to significant data compromises and financial penalties.

The Subtle Shift Towards Ethical Compromise

Often, ethical compromises begin subtly. Small decisions made under pressure can lead to a culture where questionable practices become normalized. Over time, this can erode the moral fabric of an organization, leading to more significant issues.

Personal Growth and Ethical Choices

1. Recognizing the Comfort Zone

It's easy to settle into routines that feel safe but may not align with one's values or aspirations. Real growth begins the moment you realize you're stuck in your comfort zone.

2. Embracing Challenges

Stepping out of familiar patterns can be daunting, but it's essential for personal and professional development. Embracing new challenges, even when they come with risks, can lead to greater fulfillment and success.

Charting a Course Forward

Understanding past corporate missteps provides valuable lessons for the future. By fostering a culture of integrity, encouraging open communication, and being willing to step out of comfort zones, individuals and organizations can navigate challenges more effectively and build a more ethical and resilient workplace.

"Integrity is doing the right thing, even when no one is watching." – C.S. Lewis

Consider a scenario where an employee notices a minor discrepancy in financial reporting. Addressing it promptly, rather than overlooking it, can prevent potential larger issues down the line and reinforce a culture of accountability.

Breaking Free from the Corporate Whirlpool: Turning Stagnation into Growth

We've all felt it, that feeling of being pulled in every direction, stuck in the same place, doing the same things, while knowing deep down that we want more. Welcome to the corporate whirlpool, a place where routines replace risks, where fear outweighs ambition, and where even good people can slowly drift into choices they once thought they'd never make.

But here's the truth: this whirlpool doesn't have to trap you. It can teach you how to swim smarter if you choose to break free.

What Organizations Can Do

Just like a strong current can carry someone off course, a company's culture can either pull people down or lift them up. The solution? Build workplaces where ethics and growth go hand-in-hand.

Promote Ethical Leadership

People follow what they see. Leaders must walk the talk; not just in boardroom speeches, but in everyday actions. When honesty, fairness, and accountability are modeled at the top, it sets the tone for everyone else.

"If the lighthouse flickers, the ships will crash."

Invest in People

Employees aren't robots. They need more than just salaries; they need learning, support, and a reason to grow. Simple steps like mentorship programs, growth plans, and leadership opportunities make people feel seen and valued.

What You Can Do (Yes, You!)

Whether you're a new intern, a mid-career manager, or a seasoned leader, we all face moments where we must decide; do I play it safe, or do I step up?

Take Calculated Risks

Think about the times you said no to something new because it felt scary. Now ask yourself: what did you miss by not trying? Growth lives outside the comfort zone.

"The biggest risk is thinking you're not ready."

Find a Mentor

Every great swimmer had a coach. Find someone who's a few steps ahead of you. Talk to them, learn from their mistakes, and let them show you that you're not alone.

The Ripple Effect of Doing the Right Thing

When you choose to stick to your values, even when it's tough, you don't just grow professionally. You grow as a person. It strengthens your identity, builds trust, and earns you the kind of respect no title can give.

And when organizations create cultures that reward integrity instead of shortcuts, they unlock something powerful: people who actually care.

Example: Sarah, a mid-level HR professional, was once asked to "ignore" a complaint about a senior leader's behavior. Instead of brushing it aside, she raised it, politely but firmly. It wasn't easy. But her courage led to a policy review, better training, and a culture shift in her team. Today, she leads that very department.

The price of integrity may be high, but its value lasts forever.

Don't Let the Whirlpool Define You

It's easy to get stuck in the routine, to quietly let things slide, or to stay still because it feels safe. But growth only happens when you decide to move; when you ask the hard questions, take a stand, or try something new.

You're not just a cog in a machine. You're the captain of your boat. Whether you drift or drive is up to you.

"A whirlpool spins in circles. Your life shouldn't."

4 HUMAN BEHAVIOR IN CRISIS AND COMFORT: UNDERSTANDING OUR PSYCHOLOGICAL RESPONSES

Crisis or Comfort? Why We Do What We Do

Ever wondered why we freeze up when something goes wrong or why we avoid doing something new even if we know it might help us grow?

Well, it's not just "you being you." It's actually how the human brain is wired. Whether you're a teacher, an engineer, a homemaker, or a business leader, we all face this inner tug-of-war between stepping up or staying safe. And understanding why we behave the way we do can change the way we handle life's highs and lows.

Why Do We Freeze? – Fight, Flight… or Just Float?

We've all heard of "fight or flight." But there's another reaction that's just as common, it's called the "float" mode.

Let's say your boss suddenly asks you to lead a major presentation. You don't fight. You don't run. You just sit there, nod, and silently hope it goes away. That's floating, mentally checking out, delaying action, or avoiding decisions when the pressure feels too much.

The Science Bit (Simplified):

- It is your brain's alarm system, the amygdala, that first reacts when fear shows up
- But when things get too much, your thinking brain (prefrontal cortex) stalls
- So instead of acting, you pause… and sometimes, freeze entirely

"It is not the storm that sinks the ship. It is the silence in the captain's cabin"

The Titanic Moment – A Real-World 'Float' Story

In 1912, when the Titanic hit the iceberg, many passengers didn't rush to the lifeboats. Not because they didn't care, but because they couldn't process what was happening. That hesitation? A classic float response.

Think about it: how often have you seen warning signs but stayed still, be it in a toxic relationship, a sinking project, or a business idea going nowhere?

Comfort Zones – Safe or Silent Killers?

The comfort zone feels like a cozy couch on a rainy day; you don't want to leave it. But if you sit there too long, you forget how to move.

Example: Meet Brian. Mid-40s, stable job, good pay, zero excitement. Every time a new opportunity popped up, he said, "Maybe next year." Ten years passed. Same desk. Same story.

"Comfort isn't always kind; it just hides the cracks in your potential."

Stepping Up in a Storm – Crisis Creates Leaders

Not everyone freezes. Some use the crisis to act. Like 'Indra Nooyi' during the 2008 crisis. While many CEOs played it safe, she made bold moves to reshape PepsiCo's future. It paid off. She didn't float; she navigated.

You don't need a global crisis to prove yourself. Even volunteering for a new task, giving honest feedback, or helping a struggling colleague is a brave step out of your comfort zone.

When Teams Float – The Innovation Stagnation

A product team in a large company kept launching "safe" versions of the same products. No bold ideas. No real excitement.

Their manager shook things up:

- Monthly role rotations
- Collaborations with unfamiliar departments
- Customer field visits
- Presentations outside their skill zone

At first, it was chaos. But within six months? Productivity soared. Innovation bounced back.

"Growth starts where your routine ends."

Small Town Dreamer, Anita's Leap

Anita ran a tiny bakery in her hometown. Her cookies were amazing, but she feared expanding. What if she failed?

One mentor encouraged her, and she secured a loan and launched a small chain. Her risk paid off.

"Your dreams won't chase you back. You've got to run toward them."

What You Can Do Today

If You're Stuck:

- Say "yes" to one thing that frightens you
- Start a hobby you've been delaying
- Talk to someone doing what you wish you could

If You're Leading a Team:

- Rotate responsibilities for fresh perspectives
- Encourage open feedback without fear
- Celebrate small risks, not just big wins

Don't Just Survive, Navigate

Crisis and comfort are both part of life. But whether you float or move forward is your choice.

Learn what your brain is doing, but don't let it always have the last word.

"You're not stuck. You're just waiting for permission to start swimming. Give it to yourself."

SECTION II –

DECODING THE DRIFT

5 THE HYPOTHESIS: WHY DO WE ESCAPE?

In the modern corporate jungle, where deadlines roar louder than ambitions and change knocks before you're ready, the idea of "escaping" is not always about running away; it's often about mentally retreating.

This subtle yet powerful drift is what we metaphorically call "The Escape Boat." It's not a vehicle of rescue; it's a psychological lifeboat built from excuses, rationalizations, and emotional self-defense.

Escape is not always a physical act; it's a mental retreat. We flee from opportunities that demand risk, discomfort, or change because our brains perceive uncertainty as a threat.

Why Do We Choose Comfort Over Growth?

The human mind is wired for survival, not just in the physical sense but also in the psychological realm. When faced with uncertainty, our instinct is often to retreat; to board "The Escape Boat" and drift away from challenges rather than confront them.

But what fuels this escape? Are we stuck because of real challenges, or because of the excuses we believe?

The Anatomy of the Escape Boat

The Escape Boat is not a physical structure; it's a state of mind. It is crafted from our fears, insecurities, and resistance to change. It's the place we go when faced with opportunities that ask us to be uncomfortable, to stretch, risk, or transform.

When life throws a chance our way that feels bigger than our current self-image, we often don't leap forward; we build the boat and drift away.

People navigating this mental boat paddle away from opportunities using familiar phrases:

- "I'm not ready yet."
- "I don't have enough experience."
- "This isn't the right time."
- "Why are we getting people from outside?"
- "Is there a threat to accept, or should we collaborate? What should I do?"
- "Would someone steal my thunder?"

Each phrase is like an oar, subtly rowing them away from progress. What appears to be logic is often fear wearing a mask of reason.

Mindset Blocks vs. Situational Blocks

To understand this drift, we must separate the two forces that push us into The Escape Boat:

1. Mindset Blocks: These come from internal beliefs, like:

- "I'm not leadership material"
- "Only outspoken people get noticed"
- "I am scared that failing will make others stop believing in me"

Mindset blocks are self-imposed prisons. They are beliefs etched into our minds over years of societal conditioning, early experiences, or fear of judgment. These thoughts act as psychological paddles, pushing us further into the safety of stagnation. They require awareness, reflection, and inner work to overcome.

2. Situational barriers: are they real or just in our minds? These include genuine challenges like:

- Financial responsibilities that make risk-taking difficult

- Lack of formal education or training
- Geographical limitations or family obligations

Unlike mindset blocks, situational blocks are often tangible. However, many blend the two.

For example -
Someone might say, "I can't take this opportunity because I have no time," when, in truth, the deeper fear is of being exposed as unprepared or incompetent.

As part of a survey done by the research institute and news agency, exploring career decision-making and workplace attitudes, we gathered candid insights from professionals across various sectors:

- A healthcare worker shared, "I'm interested in moving to a digital health startup, but I worry about failing and losing the security of my current stable job."
- An employee working in a BPO expressed hesitation, saying, "I've thought about applying for a leadership position, but I'm concerned they might reject me since I don't hold a formal degree."
- A seasoned employee from a century-old company remarked, "We've always handled things internally; I don't see why we should bring in outsiders now."

These responses highlight common fears and reservations that influence career choices and openness to change, reflecting the complex interplay between ambition, risk perception, and organizational culture.

Emotional Self-Defense Mechanisms: Why We Sabotage Ourselves

Avoiding risk isn't always laziness; it's emotional self-defense. Our brain is naturally built to protect us from anything it sees as a threat. When confronted with change or challenge, it activates mechanisms to protect us from emotional pain:

1. Imposter Syndrome
   - "What if they realize I'm not as capable as they believe?"

Leads to rejecting opportunities before even trying.

2. Loss Aversion
   - We worry more about what we might lose than what we could possibly gain

     Example: Staying in a dead-end job because "better the devil you know."
3. Hyper-Caution Under the Guise of Prudence
   - "I need more data before deciding."
   - "Let me wait for the perfect moment."

Result? Infinite delay!

Breaking Free: Jumping Off The Escape Boat

1. Challenge Your Narratives (Creative Thinking)
   - Ask: "Is this a true barrier or just fear in disguise?" and stretch your mindset by challenging the status quo with small, bold steps forward

     Example: If you think "I'm not ready," ask: "What's the smallest step I can take today?"
2. Reframe Risk as Growth
   - Instead of "What if I fail?" ask "What if I succeed?"

     Example: A BPO employee afraid of leadership could start with mentoring a junior.
3. Embrace Discomfort as a Compass
   - When something both thrills and scares you, it's often a sign you should go for it

4. Differentiate Between Valid Concerns and Excuses
    - Valid: "I can't afford to quit without savings."
    - Excuse: "I'll never be good enough, so why try?"

The Escape Boat vs. Real Caution – Are You Backing Off or Being Wise?

Every day, we make decisions; some small, some life-altering. In the workplace or life, we often find ourselves stuck between taking a bold step or staying right where we are. But here's the tricky part:

Not every hesitation is a sign of weakness, and not every bold move is smart.

So, how do you know when you're protecting yourself wisely... and when you're just dodging growth?

Let's explore what it means to truly navigate decisions, especially when you're unsure whether you're being cautious or just crafting clever excuses to avoid the unknown.

The Escape Boat Metaphor: Comfort Masquerading as Logic

We've all been there; moments when we say, "Maybe this isn't the right time," or "I'm not ready yet." These are our The Escape Boats: safe, easy, and oh-so-convincing.

But the question is: Are you genuinely not ready, or are you just afraid to get uncomfortable?

"An excuse in a suit still hides fear underneath."

Spotting the Difference: Genuine Concerns vs. The Escape Boats

Understanding whether a concern is valid or just fear in disguise is crucial. Let's look at these examples:

Genuine Concerns: When Caution is Smart

Real concerns come from facts, clear thinking, and honest self-reflection. They often help in making long-term, sustainable decisions.

Technical Support Role:

Imagine Yuvi, who's been offered a promotion to team lead. He pauses, not because he's afraid, but because he lacks leadership training. He's not saying "no" out of fear; he's saying, "Let me get ready the right way." That's smart.

Travel Company Analyst:

Nancy, working in an Online Travel Agency (OTA), turns down a proposal to invest in a volatile international market. Her decision is based on a careful financial analysis, not because she's afraid, but because she knows stability matters more right now.

These aren't final "no's"; they're just "not right now" backed by reason, not fear.

The Escape Boat Thinking: When Fear Dressed Up as Logic

The Escape Boat shows up when we let fear steer the ship. We come up with justifiable-sounding reasons, but deep down, they're comfort zone clingers.

GCC Employee Avoiding Collaboration:

"Why should we involve other departments? Why does someone have to dictate to me on my work? I am not heard. They don't get our work." That sounds like a strategy, but it's fear of change and loss of control.

Tech Support Agent Avoiding Training:

"I don't have time for new courses." The reality? There's flexible time available. What's truly missing is the courage to step out and keep growing.

"The excuse is not in the calendar, but it is in the comfort zone."

Factor	Genuine Concern	The Escape Boat
Intent	Supports goals and growth	Avoids discomfort or accountability
Basis	Logical, fact-based reasoning	Emotional, fear-driven reasoning
Outcome	Leads to development opportunities	Results in stagnation or missed chances

Use Case: The Skill Audit Breakthrough

In several Global Capability Centers (GCCs), hesitation to adopt AI tools was high. Instead of pushing employees, leaders conducted skill audits to identify real capability gaps. Then, they launched a mentoring and upskilling program.

Result? A 40% drop in reluctance to embrace new tech. People weren't just told to "do better"; they were given the tools to feel ready.

Don't punish hesitation, unpack it.

How to Tell If You're Escaping or Evolving

When you catch yourself hesitating, ask:

- Is this based on facts or fears?
- What's the worst that could happen?
- Will this decision still make sense six months from now?
- Am I staying back because I'm not ready, or because I'm too comfortable?

Use tools like SWOT analysis to bring objectivity to emotional decisions.

Fostering Growth-Friendly Workplaces

Leaders, take note. You can help your teams avoid The Escape Boat behavior by:

- Creating psychological safety where it's okay to say "I'm not ready… yet"
- Offering mentorship and coaching to address real limitations
- Celebrate effort, not just outcomes, honor those who dare, not only those who succeed

Paddle Toward, Not Away

Every opportunity you face is a fork in the road. One path asks you to grow, while the other asks you to stay the same. There's no shame in caution, but don't let it become a cloak for fear.

"The shoreline of your future isn't far; it's just across the waters you're avoiding."

So next time you're hesitating, don't just ask "What if it goes wrong?" Ask instead: "What if this is exactly the step I've been waiting for?"

6 BEYOND THE EXCUSES – WHY DO WE ESCAPE AND HOW?

The Hotel Manager Who Stayed Behind the Curtain

Steve is working in the hospital industry for more than a decade. As the operations head at a luxury hotel, he was known for ensuring seamless guest experiences and mentoring junior staff with precision.

He was trusted, respected, and stuck.

When offered a regional director role overseeing five properties, Steve gently declined.

"This isn't the right time," he said.

"My family needs me here."

"I don't think I am ready for that kind of corporate pressure."

His team didn't question it. His reasons sounded thoughtful, responsible, even.

But privately, Steve was battling something deeper:

A past incident where he struggled to manage a crisis during a VIP event and was publicly reprimanded by leadership.

A fear that he wouldn't adapt to the high-stakes expectations of multi-property oversight.

A belief that his value was limited to what he already knew, not what he could grow into.

So, he stayed behind the scenes. Reliable. Safe. Unchallenged.

He wasn't choosing peace. He was choosing escape disguised as responsibility.

"Sometimes the biggest comfort is the belief that we've already given our best; when in truth, we've only tested our safest."

What Is Escape? And Why Do We Choose It?

Escape doesn't always look like running away. Often, it looks like staying exactly where we are; justifying our inaction with what sound like reasonable explanations.

People escape when:

- Fear feels bigger than opportunity
- Comfort feels safer than growth
- Failure seems more permanent than effort

Escape can be physical (quitting a job), emotional (shutting down), or even disguised as logic (repeating "Now's not the right time").

It's subtle. It's socially acceptable. And most dangerously, it's self-approved.

Root Cause Analysis: Beyond the Excuses

The Six Layers of Escape

Behind every excuse is a story, and behind that story is usually a wound. While surface-level excuses such as "I'm not ready," "It's not the right time," or "I don't have enough experience" may seem like logical reasoning, they often mask much deeper psychological patterns. These patterns form what we call the "Six Layers of Escape": invisible yet powerful forces that anchor people to inaction and drift them away from potential growth.

Root Cause Analysis (RCA), in its truest form, is not just about finding out what went wrong, but also about asking why we act the way we do. It's about peeling back the layers, one by one, to reveal the inner architecture of hesitation.

The Six Layers of Escape

We all have dreams, ambitions, and ideas that never see the light of day. We tell ourselves we're "waiting for the right time" or "need more preparation," but deep down, we know these are just excuses.

What's holding us back?

Beneath the surface of procrastination and self-sabotage lie six psychological escape routes, mental traps that keep us stuck in cycles of hesitation and regret.

Why We Hold Back: The Real Reasons Behind Playing It Safe

Have you ever found yourself hesitating to speak up in a meeting, declining an opportunity, or quietly stepping back from a challenge, even when something inside you wanted to leap?

You're not lazy. You're not unambitious.

You're likely just human, navigating deep-rooted beliefs and emotional wiring that shape your response to risk and visibility.

This isn't about lack of talent; it's about the silent, inner forces that keep us stuck in patterns of hesitation.

Let's dive into the 6 hidden anchors that make us escape or hold back, often without even realizing it.

1. Fear of Judgment; "What They Will Think of Me?"

From classrooms to boardrooms, this thought haunts many of us. Whether it's sharing an idea or stepping up for a new role, the fear of being laughed at, dismissed, or misjudged can feel bigger than the opportunity itself.

Example:
A marketing consultant at a fashion retail firm developed a brilliant digital strategy to boost customer engagement. She rewrote it five times, but it never saw daylight.

"What if the team thinks it's too bold? What if I look overconfident?"

So, she shelved it, choosing silence over risk.

Root Cause: Our minds are built to crave connection, so we often fear being judged. That fear can feel like rejection, even when no one is judging us. Most of the time, it's just our imagination creating the fear.

"We fear looking foolish, not realizing that inaction speaks louder than a failed idea."

2. Fear of Rejection; "What If I'm Not Picked?"

Rejection doesn't just bruise our ego; it hits our identity. It whispers, "You're not good enough," making us opt out before we even try.

Example:
A sous-chef at a high-end hotel was offered the chance to lead a pop-up event. Instead of grabbing it, he declined.

"I'd rather not step up and get shot down. What if they regret picking me?"

He stayed in the kitchen while someone less experienced seized the spotlight.

Root Cause: Rejection feels personal. But often, a "no" is about timing or fit, not worth.

"Rejection doesn't define your worth; it refines your direction."

3. Impostor Syndrome: "Am I Even Supposed to Be Here?"

Even successful people struggle with a nagging sense that they've fooled everyone, and they're about to be found out.

Example:
A senior financial advisor at a wealth management firm shared:

"Despite managing portfolios worth millions, I still feel like a fraud when sitting with ultra-high-net-worth clients."

This self-doubt didn't match her results, but it controlled her voice in key decisions.

Root Cause: When identity lags behind achievements, confidence doesn't catch up. We need permission from ourselves to grow into our new levels.

"Confidence isn't the absence of doubt, but the decision to move anyway."

4. Scarcity Mindset: "If They Win, I Lose"

Some people view opportunities like slices of a limited pie; if someone else gets more, they get less. This mindset limits collaboration, generosity, and innovation.

Example:
At a large hotel chain, two department heads avoided sharing best practices.

"Why should I help them streamline their process? They'll get the credit."

The result? Siloed growth, internal friction, and missed collective wins.

Root Cause: Scarcity is often rooted in past loss or insecurity. It frames success as competitive, not collaborative.

"Value grows when shared. There's more pie when we bake together."

5. Toxic Comparison: "They're Miles Ahead, So Why Try?"

Scrolling through LinkedIn or watching your peers excel can spark not inspiration, but inadequacy. We compare our messy middle to someone else's highlight reel.

Example:
A young architect constantly measured herself against her peers who had international awards.

"Even if I do well here, I'm still behind. What's the point?"

She stopped submitting her designs for competitions entirely.

Root Cause: Social comparison is natural, but when it overrides self-worth, it breeds paralysis.

"Your race isn't lost just because someone else started earlier."

6. Learned Helplessness: “Nothing I Do Makes a Difference”

Repeated setbacks can make us believe our actions don’t matter. Over time, this creates emotional numbness and detachment.

Example:
A resort guest relations officer said:

“Every time I propose a change, it gets ignored. So now, I just do what I am asked to do.”

Even when new leadership arrived, she stayed silent, convinced nothing would change.

Root Cause: When effort doesn’t seem to equal impact, we internalize powerlessness. But patterns change when approached with new awareness.

> “The past is not a prophecy; unless we keep living it.”

What Ties It All Together?

We often mistake hesitation as laziness or lack of willpower. In reality, it's often an emotional defense mechanism, protecting us from past pain, shame, or fear.

Instead of asking, “Why am I stuck?” ask:

“What am I trying to protect myself from?”

That’s where clarity begins. That’s where growth happens.

RETHINK: From Excuses to Awareness

Let’s not call them "excuses" anymore. Let’s call them what they are:

Unspoken Stories That Deserve Empathy and Exploration

"When we recognize what's holding us back emotionally and shift the stories we tell ourselves, we stop running and start rising.".

So next time you find yourself holding back, pause and ask:

"Is this a red light… or just a foggy windshield?"

Breaking Free of the Drift

Every excuse has roots. And like tangled roots under the surface of still water, they go deep and intertwine. Escaping The Escape Boat isn't about brute force; it's about gentle excavation. By understanding these six layers:

1. We stop labelling ourselves as lazy or fearful
2. We start seeing patterns, not flaws
3. And we give ourselves the compassion and clarity to act; deliberately, bravely, and without apology

Because the opposite of escape isn't survival; it's ownership.

Breaking the Pattern: Turning Escapes into Encounters

Here's how to shift from escape to engagement:

1. Name the Real Fear

What are you truly afraid of: judgment, failure, being exposed? Naming it gives you power over it.

2. Use the 3 WHYs Rule

Ask yourself:

- Why am I saying no?
- Why does that reason feel safe?
- Why am I okay staying stuck?

The third answer is where truth begins.

3. Create Micro-Wins

Take small steps outside your escape zone. Speak at a team meeting before a conference. Lead a mini-project for a department.

4. Find an Anchor (Mentor or Peer)

Having someone who believes in you helps you challenge your escape narratives.

5. Reframe Mistakes as Feedback

Failure doesn't mean you're not capable. It means you're collecting data to get better.

The Escape Boat: Excuses or Valid Reasons?

Imagine excuses as an "Escape Boat." When faced with uncertainty, we jump into this boat to avoid discomfort and risk. While it may offer temporary relief, it also prevents us from reaching the shore of success.

To overcome this tendency, we must challenge our excuses and distinguish between genuine obstacles and fears disguised as reasons.

Escape is Easy, Engagement is Empowering

Sometimes, avoiding risk feels smart, like saying, 'Now isn't the right time, ' but often, it's just fear pretending to be reason.

But real growth begins when you stay in the moment, look your fears in the eye, and say:

"I may not be ready, but I'm willing."

So next time you're tempted to say "Not now," ask:

Is this a pause for preparation… or am I just politely stepping away from my potential?

"You can't reach your destiny while rowing away from it."

7 THE INTERNAL WEATHER REPORT

Tools for Self-Awareness and Behavioral Mapping

Most of us wake up each day checking the weather forecast: cloudy, sunny, stormy, so we can plan how to dress or travel. Yet, how often do we check our internal weather?

Like the skies, our emotions, thoughts, and mental states shift daily. Some days we feel energetic and optimistic; others are clouded by fear, frustration, or self-doubt. These emotional climates influence our decisions, especially the ones we postpone, avoid, or walk away from. In corporate life, this inner turbulence often becomes "The Escape Boat" mechanism, a behavioral pattern where we dodge discomfort through distraction, excuses, or silent withdrawal.

The "Internal Weather Report" is a self-awareness tool to help professionals tune into their emotional environment, map behavioral responses, and recognize escape patterns before they hijack opportunity or growth.

Just as meteorologists predict storms by analyzing atmospheric patterns, we can forecast our emotional and behavioral tendencies by observing our "Internal Weather." This self-awareness helps us:

- Recognize escape patterns (e.g., procrastination, self-doubt) before they derail us
- Identify causes that change our mindset (stress, criticism, comparison)
- Interrupt autopilot reactions and choose intentional responses

In the workplace, unchecked internal climates can:

- Affects how we respond to challenges and feedback
- Distort how we view risk and failure

- Influence whether we speak up or stay silent
- Trigger automatic "escape" responses (deflection, over-rationalizing, procrastination)

Being aware of your internal weather gives you back control; it creates a gap between stimulus and response, giving space for conscious action.

Tools for Self-Awareness and Behavioral Mapping

1. Emotional Thermometer (Inspired by the Mood Meter - Marc Brackett, Yale University)

Track emotional fluctuations and their catalysts.

Rate your emotions daily by checking:

- Energy Level (1–10)
- Pleasantness (1–10)
- Focus (1–10)

Ask yourself:

- What triggered today's emotional temperature?
- How did it affect my decision-making or communication?

Activity

For one week:

- Emotion (e.g., frustration, anxiety, excitement)
- Trigger (e.g., "boss micromanaged me," "saw a peer's promotion post")
- Behavioural Response (e.g., procrastinated, overworked, withdrew)

Example (Activity Template):

Date	Emotion (1-10 intensity)	Trigger	My Response	Escape Pattern? (e.g., avoidance, overthinking)
Mon 10th	Anxiety (7)	Upcoming presentation	Scrolled social media for 2 hrs	Avoidance
Tue 11th	Frustration (5)	Team ignored the suggestion	Complained to a coworker	Learned Helplessness

2. The Escape Pattern Detector

This helps you track common behaviours when discomfort arises.

Look for:

- Avoidance (Procrastination, Diversion)
- Emotional Outburst (Irritation, Withdrawal)
- Intellectualizing (Over-explaining why you didn't act)
- Delegating upwards (Passing the baton unnecessarily)
- Blaming external factors (System, policy, market, others)

Activity:

Identify which of the **Six Layers of Escape** (fear of judgment, impostor syndrome, etc.) dominate your behaviour.

Step 1: Recall Recent Challenges

Think of 3 situations where you:

- Avoided taking action
- Felt stuck or resistant

- Made excuses (e.g., "I'll do it later")

Step 2: Analyze the Underlying Escape Mechanism

Use this Escape Pattern Checklist:

Situation	Excuse I Told Myself	Escape Layer (Six Layers)	What I Felt
Didn't apply for promotion	"I'm not qualified enough"	Impostor Syndrome	Self-doubt
Avoided networking event	"They won't like me"	Fear of Rejection	Anxiety

Step 3: Spot the Trend

- Which escape layer appears most?
- What emotions fuel it? (Shame? Fear? Insecurity?)

Visual Reminder: Use sticky notes to label recurring patterns on your workspace as pictorial reminders

3. The Thought-Feeling-Behavior Loop

This builds a conscious map of how your internal narrative shapes your real-world choices.

Write down:

- The situation (e.g., new project offered)
- Your thoughts about it
- Your emotional response
- The action or inaction that followed

Activity:
The "Internal Weather" Forecast Worksheet

Predict and prepare for mindset shifts

Current Forecast (Right Now):

- **Primary Emotion: _____**
- **Dominant Escape Pattern: _____**
- **Physical Sensation: (e.g., tight chest, fatigue) _____**

Storm Warnings (Triggers to Watch For):

- When _____ happens, I typically respond by _____.
- My "go-to" escape behavior is _____.

Clear Skies Strategy (Intervention Plan):

- If [*trigger*] occurs, I will [*action*]:

Example: "*If I feel impostor syndrome before a meeting, I'll review my 'evidence file' of past wins.*"

- Emergency Reset: A 5-minute grounding technique (e.g., box breathing, power pose)

Activity: Identify Your Escape Patterns
Recognize how, when, and why you retreat into "The Escape Boat."

Step-by-Step Instructions

1. Pick a Recent Opportunity or Challenge

Something you avoided, declined, or procrastinated on

E.g., a leadership opportunity, a public speaking task, or an innovation pitch

2. **Write the Scenario in Detail**
    - What happened?
    - What were you asked or expected to do?

3. **Complete the Internal Weather Report (Template below)**
    - Use the Emotional Thermometer
    - Reflect on your thoughts, feelings, behaviours

4. **Map the Escape Pattern**
    - Which pattern did you follow (avoidance, blame, etc.)?
    - What was the internal reason?

5. **Reframe with Clarity**
    - If you had another chance, what choice would you make if you were bold and fully aware?

Template: Internal Weather Report & Escape Pattern Map

Parameter	Your Reflection
Situation/ Opportunity	Describe what happened
Emotional Energy (1–10)	
Pleasantness (1–10)	
Focus Level (1–10)	
Primary Thought	
Emotion Felt	
Action Taken	
Escape Pattern Observed	(Avoidance, Excuse-making, Overthinking, etc.)
Root Cause Layer	(Fear of Rejection, Impostor Syndrome, etc.)
Conscious Reframe	"If I had to respond today, what would a courageous step look like?"

Ask yourself:

- When do I most often retreat into excuses?
- What emotional weather frequently triggers my Escape Boat?
- Which colleagues or environments activate my discomfort patterns?
- What would it look like to show up with clarity instead of fear?

Use Case: A product manager at a mid-sized tech firm shared:

"When I was offered the chance to lead a cross-functional initiative, I initially said no. I told them I was too swamped. But when I used the internal weather check-in later, I realized I felt exposed and unsure. I didn't want to fail in front of senior leaders. That self-check helped me call back and say yes. It became one of the most fulfilling projects I've done."

The weather inside matters more than the weather outside. Learning to read your internal patterns helps you break the autopilot response, reclaim agency, and align action with intention. With practice, The Escape Boat will no longer be your refuge; it will become your reflection point.

You can't change the weather, but you can carry an umbrella.
What's your emotional umbrella?

SECTION III –

THE TRANSFORMATION STRATEGY

8 ANCHORING AWARENESS

"Opportunity Never Knocks the Door the Second Time – Grab it When It Comes" – Like a Dodo bird

Opportunities rarely present themselves twice. The adage, "Opportunity never knocks the door the second time, grab it when it comes," is more than a motivational slogan; it's a call to action rooted in both psychology and real-world outcomes. Yet, many people, influenced by "The Escape Boat" mindset, hesitate or retreat, missing out on life-changing chances. The path to breaking this cycle begins with a transformation strategy grounded in self-awareness and emotional literacy.

Anchoring awareness serves as the bedrock for personal and organizational change, paving the path for transformation through the understanding of opportunities and emotions. Anchoring awareness not only opens the door to action but also ensures that individuals and organizations are aligned with the call for change at the right moment.

From Escape to Embrace

Every day in professional and personal life, we stand at crossroads. These are moments of decision;

Should I speak up?

Should I accept that opportunity?

Should I initiate that conversation or wait for 'the right time'?

Often, we hesitate. And The Escape Boat, our mind's crafted excuse machine, gently pulls us back into a zone of comfort. What we don't realize is that many of these crossroads are opportunities disguised as discomfort. And like a train that doesn't loop back, they don't always return.

Anchoring Awareness: The First Step Toward Change

'Transformation doesn't start with action; it starts with awareness.'

Building self-awareness is where real change begins. This means cultivating a clear, honest understanding of your internal state; your thoughts, emotions, and habitual reactions when faced with opportunity or risk. Research shows that people who believe opportunities are fixed (unchangeable) are more likely to adopt passive strategies, such as waiting or hoping for another chance, rather than acting decisively. In contrast, those with a growth mindset see opportunities as cultivable and are more likely to take action, even when the path isn't clear.

Change begins with awareness, acknowledging the need for transformation and understanding the opportunities around us. Often, life presents a fleeting chance, and it is our ability to anchor our awareness to those moments that determines the trajectory of success. The phrase "Opportunity never knocks on the door the second time" urges us to stay vigilant, open-minded, and willing to act when change is within reach.

For instance, in the realm of business transformation, an organization at a crossroads might recognize a market shift as an opportunity to diversify its product range. Amazon's early pivot from being an online bookstore to an e-commerce giant exemplifies this principle. Jeff Bezos, recognizing the evolving digital landscape, anchored awareness within his team and acted decisively, transforming a singular opportunity into a revolution in online shopping. This ability to see and seize opportunities, driven by clear awareness, was the first step in creating a lasting impact.

On a personal level, consider an individual striving for professional growth. Suppose an employee is offered a chance to lead a small project outside their usual role. Anchoring their awareness to this opportunity as a springboard to build leadership skills can shape their career progression. Those who hesitate or overthink often miss such critical chances, as these moments rarely present themselves again.

Just like a ship needs an anchor to steady itself before it changes direction, humans need to anchor their awareness before they can navigate transformation. It starts with taking a moment to observe what's driving you, whether it's fear, hesitation, hope, or habit.

"Until you make the unconscious conscious, it will direct your life and you will call it fate."; Carl Jung

In corporate life, we call it "bad luck" when we miss a promotion. In personal life, we say, "Maybe it wasn't meant to be." But often, the truth is: we weren't present or brave enough to recognize the opportunity when it came knocking.

Anchoring awareness often requires mindfulness exercises, journaling key observations, or regular strategic reflections on potential growth areas. These habits heighten awareness and prepare individuals to act swiftly when an opportunity arises.

Example:

Consider two equally skilled professionals who miss out on a promotion. The first, believing "another chance will come," waits passively, hoping for luck to turn. The second, recognizing that the same door may not open again, seeks feedback, builds new skills, and networks actively; often creating new opportunities in the process. Over time, research confirms that the latter approach leads to greater goal attainment and resilience

Anchoring awareness means pausing to ask:

- What am I feeling right now?
- Am I hesitating out of genuine caution or out of fear?
- Should I move forward now, or is this a time to pause and think?

Thinking deeply like this helps you avoid running away from challenges and start noticing chances before they slip away.

Emotional Literacy: The Silent Power Behind Real Change

We often talk about strategy, execution, and leadership when it comes to transformation, whether at work or in life. But there's one silent force that determines whether change truly sticks or quietly slips away:

Emotional Literacy: the ability to recognize, understand, and manage your emotions and those of others.

As Dr. Daniel Goleman, renowned psychologist and author of Emotional Intelligence, explains:

> "Self-awareness is the cornerstone of emotional and leadership growth."

This isn't just about being 'in touch with your feelings', it's about being in command of your reactions, your mindset, and how you relate to others when life throws a curveball.

What Is Emotional Literacy in Simple Terms?

Imagine your emotions are like traffic lights.

- If you know what each signal means, you can drive safely
- If you don't recognize them, you'll either crash or stall

Emotional literacy is like learning to read those signals, so you can move forward with clarity instead of confusion.

Why Emotional Literacy Is Non-Negotiable in Any Change Journey

Whether you're navigating a career pivot, leading a team through a merger, managing a health crisis, or adjusting to a new life phase, emotions are always involved.

Here's what emotional literacy helps you do:

1. Spot When Fear Is Pretending to Be Logic

Ever talked yourself out of something great with "rational reasons"?

Chances are, fear was whispering in disguise.

Use Case: A sales professional says, "This product isn't ready for launch," but deep down, they're afraid of public rejection. Emotional literacy helps identify this fear and take action anyway, with better preparation.

2. Understand How Insecurity Can Cloud Your Choices

When we feel "not good enough," we either freeze, overcompensate, or quit too soon.

Use Case: A teacher avoids applying for a leadership role at school, not because she lacks skill, but because she doubts her worth. Emotional literacy helps her name that feeling and not let it control the decision.

3. Feel Your Feelings Without Being Ruled by Them

Instead of reacting impulsively or shutting down, emotionally literate people pause, name what they feel, and choose their response.

"When you can name it, you can tame it."

Emotional Literacy at Work: The Real Leadership Differentiator

Great leaders aren't just good at strategy, they're emotionally fluent.

They understand what's not being said, and they help their teams feel seen, heard, and safe, even during chaos.

Example:
During a company-wide downsizing, one leader addresses the team:

"I know many of you are worried. I don't have all the answers yet, but I promise to be transparent and hear you out."

This creates psychological protection, a key element for engagement and trust.

Goleman's studies show that emotionally intelligent leaders drive higher morale, stronger collaboration, and better performance, even in high-pressure environments.

Emotional Literacy at Home: The Foundation of Real Connection

It's not just for the workplace. Emotional literacy shapes how we communicate with partners, parents, and kids, especially during tough transitions.

Example:
A family has the opportunity to move abroad for better prospects. The teenager resists, fearing loss of friends and familiarity.

An emotionally literate parent doesn't just say, "You'll be fine."

Instead, they say:
"I hear that you're scared to leave your friends. That makes sense. Let's talk about how we can stay connected and what new adventures might look like."

This builds trust, reduces resistance, and makes everyone feel part of the journey.

How Emotional Literacy Builds Resilience and Opportunity

When you're emotionally literate:

- You bounce back faster from failure
- You embrace growth rather than avoid it
- You connect deeply, not just communicate

It's not about suppressing emotions; it's about owning them without letting them own you.

"Change isn't hard because it's technical.
It's hard because it's emotional."

And emotional literacy is the bridge.

So next time you face a crossroad, don't just ask:

"What should I do?"

Ask:

"What am I feeling, and what is that feeling trying to teach me?"

The Inner Benefit: Confidence Without Ego

One of the biggest breakthroughs of emotional literacy is how it reshapes our inner dialogue.

You stop seeing fear as a warning siren and start seeing it as a signal, one you can work with.

You realize:

- Anxiety doesn't mean stop
- Doubt doesn't mean no
- Nervousness doesn't mean you're not ready; it means you care

Fear is not a red light. It's a blinking yellow; slow down, assess, and move forward mindfully!

Even Kids Know the Power of Naming Emotions

As highlighted by CASEL (Collaborative for Academic, Social, and Emotional Learning), children who learn to name their emotions early are better learners, problem-solvers, and collaborators.

So, imagine the advantage adults gain when they apply the same logic:

When you know what you're feeling, it's easier to choose how to respond.

The Missed Launch

Sonia, a mid-level marketing manager in a consumer goods company, was invited to co-lead a new product launch. It was a high-visibility project, something she had always wanted. But she hesitated; "What if I mess up? I don't have experience managing cross-functional teams." She politely declined.

Six months later, the same project lead that she had declined was promoted. Sonia remained in the same role. That was her train, and it didn't return.

When she reflected, she realized it wasn't lack of skill. It was a lack of self-awareness about how much fear had shaped her decision. The Escape Boat, disguised as "self-assessment", had set sail again.

Anchoring Awareness Activity: Emotional Weather Log

Identify emotional patterns that trigger escape behaviors.

Day	Situation	Emotion Felt	Thought at the Time	Action Taken	Was it Escape or Embrace?
Mon	Asked to present to leadership	Anxiety	"I'm not the best at this"	Delayed prep	Escape
Tue	Feedback from the team	Embarrass-ment	"They don't respect me"	Became passive	Escape
Wed	Offered a side project	Excitement + Fear	"What if I fail?"	Accepted it	Embrace

Repeat for 21 days. This habit will anchor awareness before the escape mechanism kicks in.

Opportunity: It Doesn't Shout; It Whispers

The thing about life-changing opportunities?

They don't arrive with flashing signs. They come softly:

- A comment from a colleague
- An open door in a meeting
- A job opening you weren't "sure" about
- A challenge that feels slightly too big

But if you're too caught up in fear, doubt, or emotional autopilot, you'll walk right past them.

Think About It:

"Opportunities aren't always loud. Sometimes, they're a quiet suggestion that disappears if ignored."

Catch the Dodo Bird Before It Vanishes

As Om Sharma puts it:

"Grab the Dodo bird in the first go; it never comes back."

That opportunity may not knock again.
That idea may not wait around.
That moment of courage might fade if you don't use it.

"Luck is what happens when preparation meets opportunity."- Lucius Annaeus Seneca, a Roman philosopher

And emotional literacy? That's your preparation.
It helps you stay calm enough to see the chance…
…and clear enough to take it.

Ask yourself today, not just "What do I want to achieve?"
But also:

"How am I feeling, and how might that feeling be shaping my next step?"

Because when your emotions are understood, not ignored, you're not just reacting; you're leading your life from the inside out.

Why This Matters: Some Windows Open Only Once

Life rarely sends a calendar invite for the moments that matter most. Opportunities often arrive unannounced, quiet, fast, and fleeting.

Research by O'Keefe and colleagues confirms a powerful truth:

Individuals who believe opportunities are rare are more likely to act.

They don't wait for the "perfect time" or a "better moment."

They understand that this moment might be the only one.

Think about it:

- That job role you considered "too big"
- That idea you didn't pitch
- That client you didn't call back
- That course you postponed

What if that was your moment, and it won't circle back?

Simple Habits That Lead to Big Change

Transformation doesn't happen overnight.
It starts with small shifts, daily awareness, better self-talk, and honest action.

Here are four practical ways to prepare for life's quiet knocks:

1. Check in With Yourself Every Day

Take 2 minutes each morning or before a big decision.
Ask yourself:

- What am I feeling right now?
- Is this emotion helping me grow or holding me back?

Why this works: You stop running on autopilot and start making conscious choices.

2. Use a Richer Emotional Language

Saying "I'm fine" hides the truth. Try using more precise words:

- Instead of bad, try overwhelmed, disappointed, or uncertain
- Instead of good, try motivated, curious, or grateful

Why this works: Specific feelings guide better actions.
Saying "I feel anxious" opens space for courage. Saying "I'm off" leads nowhere.

3. Catch the Escape Mentality

We often confuse discomfort with danger. Learn to notice when you're backing out just to stay safe.
Ask yourself:

> "Am I avoiding real risk, or just dodging discomfort?"

Use Case: A marketing professional hesitates to suggest a campaign idea during a leadership meeting. Not because the idea is weak, but because they fear judgment. Recognizing this emotional pattern allows them to speak up and stand out.

4. Act Now, Even if Small

Opportunities rarely wait. Instead of planning for months, take a tiny first step:

- Send that email
- Book that meeting
- Say "yes" to that stretch role
- Sign up for that course

You don't need perfect timing. You need purposeful timing.

Awareness Is Your Superpower

When you learn to tune in, not tune out, you stop missing chances that could shape your future.

Emotional awareness isn't about overthinking.

It's about feeling clearly, acting bravely, and staying grounded when the door creaks open.

And here's what's powerful:

People who master these micro-skills not only recognize opportunities; they create them.

Daily Anchor Statement

Write a sentence that reminds you of your power.
Something that keeps you grounded and bold.

Example:
"Today, I choose presence over panic. I will listen to my thoughts, welcome my feelings, and show up, even if I feel unsure. I won't miss my moment."

Read it every morning. Make it your compass.

Reflect On:

"What if the moment you're waiting for is already here, but you're too distracted to see it?"

Be present. Be emotionally aware. Be ready.

9 DESIGNING OPPORTUNITY READINESS: BUILDING A BIAS TOWARD ACTION

Many of us sit on brilliant ideas, meaningful goals, or long-held dreams, waiting. Waiting for the right time, the right confidence, or a perfect plan. But often, that "perfect moment" never comes. What truly separates action-takers from daydreamers isn't talent or resources, it's mindset.

Opportunity Readiness is about preparing yourself not just with plans, but with the willingness to move, even when conditions aren't ideal. It's the quiet courage to act, to test, to try before everything feels 100% safe.

What Is a Bias Toward Action?

A bias toward action is the habit of doing. Not reckless action, but thoughtful motion, testing ideas, making progress through small steps, and learning along the way. It's about saying: "I may not know everything yet, but I'm ready to start."

This idea is at the heart of Design Thinking, a method widely used in innovation and product development. Rather than waiting for a perfect blueprint, teams build prototypes, test fast, fail small, and improve quickly.

Example:
A young content creator hesitated to launch her podcast because she didn't have the perfect mic, studio, or intro music. But then she decided to just start with her phone and a silent room. Five episodes later, she had built confidence, grown an audience, and earned her first brand partnership. She didn't wait for readiness, she created it.

Why Do We Hesitate?
The basis of hesitation often isn't lack of skill; it is fear. Fear of being judged. Fear of failing. Fear of not being enough. So instead of stepping forward, we build elaborate stories about why "now's not the right time."

This is "The Escape Boat" in action, a psychological life raft we jump onto to avoid discomfort. But in doing so, we drift away from opportunities that could have transformed us.

"Opportunities don't disappear. They just move on to those who are ready to say yes."

Build Opportunity Readiness: Practical Ways to Start

- Start Before You're Fully Ready

  Take one small step today, write the email, make the call, submit the idea. Progress creates confidence

- Redefine Risk

  Ask yourself, "What is the cost of not acting?" Many a times, the risk of regret is more than the risk of failure

- Celebrate Experiments, Not Just Wins

  Every action teaches you something. Even if it doesn't work out, you're still further ahead than you were yesterday

- Shift from "All or Nothing" to "One Thing Now"

  You don't have to have everything planned; just concentrate on taking the next best step.

A Relatable Analogy

Think of opportunity as a train pulling into a station. It doesn't honk twice. If you're not ready, it doesn't wait. But here's the truth: there's always another train, if you've been preparing to board. Opportunity readiness isn't about being lucky. It's about being willing.

Your future doesn't begin with a big leap; it begins with a tiny yes. Say yes to momentum

Say yes to action

And when opportunity knocks, don't just stand there, walk through the door

Why We Resist Action (And How to Fix It)

Our brains are wired to overestimate risk and underestimate our ability to handle it.

Common thought traps include:

- "What if I fail?" → But what if you succeed?
- "I need more preparation." → Completed is better than perfect
- "It's not the right time." → There is never a "perfect" time

Example:
Sarah wants to switch careers but keeps delaying because she's waiting to "feel ready." Meanwhile, her colleague Jake jumps into a new role with only 70% confidence, and learns on the job.

The Solution?
Teach yourself to take tiny, low-risk steps; these small actions help you grow braver and gain momentum.

How to Identify the Right Opportunity

Recognizing the right opportunity involves a combination of intuition, analysis, and alignment with your goals.

Here's a roadmap:

- Set Clear Goals: Define your short-term and long-term objectives
- Evaluate Fit: Ask, "Does this opportunity align with my skills, values, and aspirations?"
- Assess Risks: Every opportunity carries risks. Weigh these against the potential rewards

Believe in Your Intuition: Often, your inner voice can lead you in the right direction

Seek Counsel: Consult mentors or trusted individuals, but ensure their advice aligns with your vision.

Preparing to Make Quick Decisions

Quick decision-making is a skill that can be developed with practice:

- Enhance Your Knowledge: Stay informed about trends and developments in your field
- Develop a Risk Appetite: Learn to embrace uncertainty and view challenges as opportunities for growth
- Build Decision-Making Frameworks: Use tools like SWOT analysis (Strengths, Weaknesses, Opportunities, Threats) to evaluate options
- Practice Time-Bound Decisions: Set small deadlines for everyday choices to train your brain to think quickly
- Reflect on Past Decisions: Analyze your successes and failures to identify patterns in your decision-making

What is a Bias Toward Action?

A bias toward action means:

- Acting before you're 100% ready
- Making decisions with clarity, not perfection
- Valuing movement over overthinking

In behavioral science, the "action bias" suggests that people tend to prefer action over inaction when facing uncertainty, but only when they trust themselves.
(Patt & Zeckhauser, "Action Bias and Behavioral Decision-Making")

So, how do we build this trust? One tiny risk at a time.

The Missed Speaking Opportunity

David, a software engineer, had always wanted to improve his visibility at work. During a team meeting, his manager casually mentioned that someone should present their product module to a visiting client. David thought of volunteering but froze. He told himself, "Maybe next time. I haven't prepared. What if I mess up?"

The moment passed. A junior team member volunteered, did well, and got noticed.

What David missed wasn't just a speaking gig. He missed an opportunity for visibility, growth, and confidence. All because he did not feel "ready enough."

Had he practiced micro-risk taking, he would've had the inner muscle to say "yes."

The Role of Micro-Risks in Fostering Action

Taking bold leaps is often intimidating, but by practicing *micro-risk taking*, individuals can gradually overcome their hesitations. Micro-risks are small, manageable steps that push one slightly out of their comfort zone without overwhelming them with fear of failure. Over time, these calculated risks build confidence and momentum, cultivating an action-oriented habit.

The Strategy: Designing Opportunity Readiness

Being ready doesn't mean eliminating fear. It means normalizing small discomforts, so when big opportunities come, you can act instead of escape.
Let's break this down into three key pillars:

- Clarity – Recognize your excuses
- Calibration – Align risks to your current capacity
- Commitment – Take small, consistent action to expand that capacity

This is where the Micro-Risk-Taking Matrix comes into play

Activity: Micro-Risk-Taking Matrix

To create a habit of daily, low-stakes action that builds confidence, reduces fear, and rewires your response to opportunity.

Zone	Examples	Frequency	Impact
Comfort Zone	Replying to emails, finishing known tasks, and avoiding new responsibilities	Daily	No growth
Stretch Zone	Speaking in a meeting, suggesting an idea, and giving peer feedback	3x per week	Builds momentum
Risk Zone	Volunteering for a presentation, asking for mentorship, and trying a new skill	1x per week	Builds courage
Leap Zone	Applying for a higher role, launching a project, or leading a team initiative	Monthly	Break-through growth

Instructions:

- Track your actions in each zone weekly
- Reflect: "Where did I play small?" or "Where did I choose growth?"
- Set 1 Micro-Risk goal each week

Week of: ___________

Micro-Risk Chosen:

____

Why I avoided it before:

____

Action I took:

____

What I learned:

____

Will I do it again? [ ] Yes [ ] No – Why? ____________________

Psychological Insight: Why Micro-Risks Work

Our brain is designed to protect us. It equates the unknown with danger. But by intentionally taking micro-risks, we teach the brain:

"This is not life-threatening. I can handle this."

Over time, the amygdala (the fear center in our brain) reduces its alarm response. This is supported by exposure therapy, a well-established psychological approach to managing anxiety and avoidance behaviours.

This works because:

- Small wins rewire your brain to associate risk with reward, not fear

- Momentum compounds; each micro-risk makes the next one easier

- You learn that discomfort ≠ danger; it's just growth in disguise

Every opportunity is a window. It will not stay open forever. Being opportunity-ready is not about having everything figured out. It is about having enough courage to take the first step.

By training your mind to act through micro-risks, you break free from The Escape Boat and learn to row toward your success, one paddle at a time.

10 REFRAMING THE NARRATIVE

Reframing the Narrative: From "Why Me?" to "Try Me"

Dealing with New Entrants, Role Shifts, and Organizational Politics

In the journey of professional growth and navigating organizational dynamics, the way we frame our internal dialogue profoundly shapes our actions and outcomes. "The Escape Boat" mindset often traps individuals in a cycle of hesitation and retreat, fueled by thoughts like

"Why me?"

A question steeped in self-doubt and victimhood. Reframing this narrative to

"Try me"

Transforms hesitation into readiness, fear into opportunity, and resistance into resilience.

The Problem: When Change Feels Like a Threat

Imagine this: You've been in your role for years. You know the ins and outs of the system. You've built credibility and respect. Then suddenly, a new hire joins, someone with an impressive resume, big ideas, and access to leadership. You begin to feel a twinge of uncertainty.

Questions start racing:

- "Why did they hire from outside?"
- "What does this mean for my growth?"

- "Are they here to replace me?"
- "Will my contributions be overshadowed?"

This emotional spiral is natural, but it's also dangerous, especially when it's left unchecked. This is how the mind boards

The Escape Boat

The mental retreat into victimhood, blame, and withdrawal. We go from "I'm capable" to "I'm being sidelined." And we don't just lose perspective, we lose opportunity.

'Shift your situation from being a "victim of change" to an architect of collaboration'

Why Changing Your Perspective to "Let Me Try" Makes a Difference

Reframing is a psychological tool that shifts perception and mindset. Instead of viewing challenges as threats or personal burdens, reframing encourages seeing them as invitations to grow and prove one's capabilities. This shift aligns with cognitive-behavioural research, which shows that how individuals interpret events influences their motivation and behavior (Beck).

The shift in mindset that separates resilient professionals from stagnant ones is subtle but powerful.

Instead of asking:

"Why is this happening to me?"

Ask:

"What can I learn from this? What can I bring to this situation?"

This shift isn't about toxic positivity or ignoring organizational politics. It's about reclaiming agency. It's about choosing to show up as a contributor, not a casualty.

The Stories We Tell Ourselves: How Mindset Shapes Action – The Narrative Bias

As humans, we are storytellers by nature, not just in books or movies, but in how we explain everyday life to ourselves. When change shows up, like a job role shift, a new boss, or a sudden challenge, we don't always wait for all the facts. Our brain quickly fills the gaps with assumptions. Unfortunately, those assumptions often lean toward fear or self-doubt.

Psychologist Dr. Paul Watzlawick calls this "The Invented Reality." We believe the first version of the story our mind creates. But these inner stories are not always objective; they're shaped by past disappointments, old beliefs, and what we think others expect of us.

"If the story you're telling yourself is holding you back, maybe it's time to rewrite the script."

Why Some People Leap While Others Linger

Ever wonder why two people in the same situation make completely different choices? One steps up, the other steps back. The difference often lies in how they think, prepare, and perceive risk.

Let's break down what sets action-takers apart and how you can build those same habits.

1. They See Growth Where Others See Obstacles

Rather than worrying about failing, proactive people wonder, "What can I discover if I give it a shot?" This is the heart of the growth mindset, a term made well-known by Dr. Carol Dweck.

Example: A mid-career professional struggling with new software doesn't shy away; they join a weekend crash course, ask questions, and practice daily. The result? They not only gain the skill but also earn visibility and trust for their initiative.

2. They Get Comfortable with the Unknown

People who thrive don't wait for full clarity before moving forward. They act even when things are unclear, knowing clarity often comes from action, not before it.

Example: A small business owner launches an eco-friendly product without knowing exactly how the market will respond. They collect early feedback, tweak the product, and build momentum gradually. Their willingness to experiment gives them an edge.

3. They Prepare When No One Is Watching

Behind every "overnight success" is quiet preparation. Action-takers invest in learning, building relationships, and staying informed, so when the right moment comes, they don't hesitate.

Example: A healthcare worker who wants to lead starts guiding new staff, picks up tech skills, and helps with projects across teams. When a leadership spot appears, they naturally stand out as the best fit.

4. They Believe in Themselves and Others

Confidence doesn't mean having all the answers. It means trusting your ability to find the answers as you go. It also means trusting others, encouraging collaboration, and creating psychological safety.

Example: A school principal facing new education policies doesn't panic. They hold open discussions with teachers, share their doubts honestly, and work through the changes as a team. This trust-based leadership boosts morale and results.

5. They Carry Authentic Gravitas

Gravitas isn't about being loud or always right. It's about being real, showing up with a mix of calm confidence, practical thinking, and humility. Rebecca Newton describes this in "Authentic Gravitas" as finding the right mix of confidence and friendliness.

Example: A community leader speaks at a town hall. Instead of pretending to know everything, they admit where more clarity is needed, but passionately stand for the community's vision. Their authenticity earns respect and rallying support.

Don't Let Your Mind Be the Roadblock!

It is not the years of experience you hold, it is about how many experiments you have done in your life and career – Om Sharma

We all have the power to choose which inner story we believe. The path to opportunity doesn't require you to be perfect; it requires you to be ready. That readiness comes from rewiring your mindset, preparing behind the scenes, and being brave enough to act even when it's hard.

"The moment you stop telling fear-based stories is the moment you start writing your future."

Why Do Opportunities Come with Limited Time?

Opportunities are products of circumstances. They are influenced by timing, external factors, and the readiness of the individual. Many times, we feel that opportunities appear suddenly because:

- **Life's Unpredictability:** Circumstances are constantly evolving, and opportunities are born from these changes. For instance, a job opening may arise when someone resigns unexpectedly
- **Lack of Preparedness:** Often, we are caught off guard because we have not anticipated change or planned for it
- **Pressure to Act Quickly:** In a fast-paced world, others may also be vying for the same opportunity, leaving little room for prolonged decision-making

To overcome this, one must cultivate a mindset of anticipation and readiness, akin to a sprinter who is always on the starting block, waiting for the signal.

Why Do We Struggle to Identify the Right Opportunities?

Opportunities are like puzzle pieces; they only fit when you know what picture you're trying to build. So why do so many of us feel lost or unsure when faced with choices?

Let's look at two often overlooked reasons: Lack of clarity and location bias.

1. Lack of Clarity: When the Destination Isn't Clear, Every Road Feels Right (or Wrong)

We often believe we've set "clear goals" or well-defined OKRs (Objective and Key Results). But here's the truth: sometimes, those goals are only surface-level; they don't reflect what truly matters to you, your team, or your organization.

Without that depth of clarity, any new opportunity may feel overwhelming. Should you go for it? Wait? Is it even right for you? Everything starts to blur.

Use Case: A team is told to "increase productivity," but no one explains how or why. So, every idea, from automation to overtime, feels like a gamble. Contrast that with a leader who co-creates the goal: "Let's reduce manual rework by 30% so we can spend more time on innovation." Now, the path is clear, and opportunity filters itself.

If you don't know what you want, how will you recognize it when it shows up?

2. Location Bias: Judging Opportunities by Where They Come from Instead of What They Offer

Location bias happens when we dismiss (or overvalue) opportunities simply because of their source.

Example 1: We may ignore a colleague's suggestion just because it came from a different department, or reject an idea because it emerged in a casual setting, not a formal strategy meeting. We might even miss life-changing insights from a junior team member or a friend outside our industry, thinking, "They don't get it."

Example 2: A startup founder gets a business idea while chatting with a cab driver. But because it didn't come from a "strategic consultant," they ignore it. Later, another company launches a similar idea, and it succeeds.

Example 3: A junior employee suggests using AI for customer support. The idea is brushed off until a high-paid consultant makes the same recommendation months later. The difference? Perceived credibility, not actual value.

Don't judge the value of an idea by the door it walks through!

The Hidden Roadblocks: Too Many Options, Too Much Noise

Add to this the flood of choices we face every day. When everything is a possibility, making the right choice becomes paralyzing. This is known as decision fatigue; the brain's way of saying, "I've had enough."

Fear of Failure: The Inner Voice That Says, "What If I Mess This Up?"

Fear is natural. But it becomes dangerous when it stops you from moving forward. Often, it's not the opportunity we doubt; it's ourselves. And this fear is especially strong when we're not encouraged to learn through trial and error.

Example: Leaders who let their team experiment (and occasionally fail) create an environment of innovation. The message is clear: "Mistakes are okay, just avoid making the same ones twice. Learn, adapt, and improve."

Influence of Others: Helpful Voices... or Hidden Barriers?

We all seek advice. But sometimes, the advice we get doesn't reflect our path. Friends and family often mean well, but they speak from their fears and expectations, not necessarily from what's best for you.

Example: A person passionate about social work is pushed by family to take up a high-paying corporate job. While the role sounds impressive on paper, it leaves them feeling empty inside. The opportunity wasn't "wrong"; it just wasn't theirs.

How to Break Free and Recognize the Right Opportunities

Start by getting real with yourself:

- What are your values?
- What skills do you enjoy using?
- What kind of challenges do you like solving?

- What outcome excites you?

When you're aligned with yourself, opportunities stop looking like risks and start feeling like doors waiting to be opened.

Opportunities don't shout. They whisper. You just need to be clear, calm, and curious enough to hear them.

Balancing Family and Career: Make Space for What Matters Without Losing Yourself

Using Prioritization Matrix and Pareto Analysis

In today's fast-paced world, juggling career goals and family responsibilities often feels like walking a tightrope. On one side is your ambition, your sense of achievement; on the other, your emotional world, your loved ones, your children, your ageing parents.

It's not a simple either-or. The real challenge is finding clarity in chaos; knowing what to say yes to, and what can wait.

This is where structured tools like the Prioritization Matrix and Pareto Analysis come in, not as cold calculations, but as guiding compasses to help you align life's decisions with your deepest values.

The Real-Life Struggle

You've been there: a crucial business meeting is scheduled the same day as your child's school performance. Or you're offered a promotion that demands relocation, while your spouse just landed their dream job in your current city.

These decisions are not just professional; they're deeply personal.

So, how do we decide wisely?

Let the Tools Guide You; Not Override You

1. The Prioritization Matrix: Choose What Counts, Not What Shouts

The Prioritization Matrix helps you sort your options based on what 'really' matters. You assess each decision against criteria like impact, effort, time, emotional cost, and alignment with your long-term goals.

Use Case Example:

You're considering taking on a high-profile project that requires long hours. Use the matrix to weigh:

- Impact on career progression
- Time away from family
- Stress level
- Personal growth
- Financial gain

You then assign scores to each factor and see clearly what outweighs what, instead of making emotional snap decisions.

Not everything urgent is important. Choose based on values, not just volume.

2. Pareto Analysis (80/20 Rule): Focus on the Few that Matter Most

Pareto Analysis is the art of simplifying. It teaches that 80% of outcomes come from 20% of actions. Apply this to your daily life, your commitments, and your stress.

Example:
If 80% of your stress comes from just 2 out of 10 tasks, let's delegate, delay, or redesign those 2. Similarly, if 80% of your family joy comes from spending just 2 hours a week of quality time, block it off like a CEO meeting.

When your time is limited, don't try to do more; try to do less, better.

What Would It Take to Be in the Value Stream?

To thrive, at work and home, you need to rise into the value stream. That means contributing to things that truly move the needle, not just checking boxes.

Tools to Help You Get There:

1. **Time-Blocking Calendar:** Schedule what matters most; work sprints, family dinner, solo recharge. If it's not on the calendar, it won't happen.
2. **Notion / Trello / Asana:** Organize your priorities visually; track progress, reduce overload, and build accountability.
3. **Reflective Journaling (Weekly Check-ins):** Write down what worked, what drained you, and what you want more of. Clarity begins with reflection.

What Does It Take to Rise into the Value Stream?

- **Self-Awareness:** Know your values, not just your tasks. Ask yourself: What do I want more of in my life? Then, filter choices accordingly

- **Boundary-Setting:** Learn to say "no" without guilt and "yes" with intention. Saying "yes" to everything is saying "no" to something else, often your peace

- **Micro-Momentum:** Don't wait for perfect conditions. Take small actions daily. One mindful step forward is better than a hundred anxious thoughts

The Prioritization Matrix

A Prioritization Matrix is a decision-making tool used to evaluate and prioritize options based on weighted criteria. It helps visualize the impact of each choice and ensures a balanced and logical approach.

You're not choosing between success or love, achievement or presence. You're building a life where both coexist. Tools like the Prioritization Matrix and Pareto Analysis don't make your decisions easier; they make them smarter.

The most important choices in life aren't between right and wrong, but between right and right. Your values decide the tie!

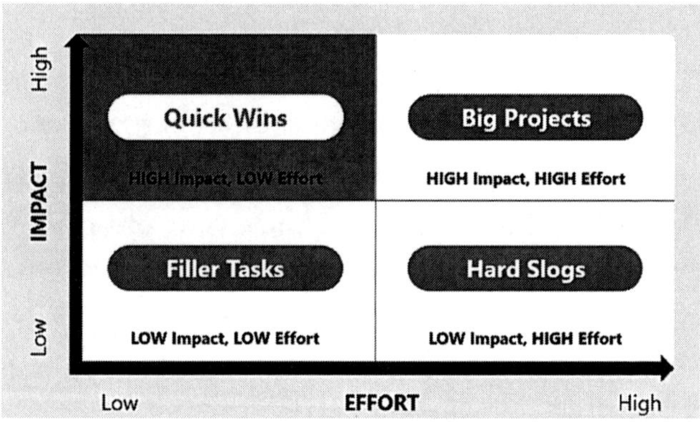

Steps to Use a Prioritization Matrix

1. **Define Criteria**

   Identify factors critical to your decision. For instance:

   For Family: Quality time, emotional well-being, support system

   For Career: Financial growth, job satisfaction, future opportunities

2. **Weight Criteria**

   Assign a weight to each criterion based on its importance or weightage

   (e.g., 1–10). Higher weight means greater importance.

3. **Score Options**

   Evaluate each option (e.g., focus on family vs. focus on career) against each criterion on a scale (e.g., 1–5).

4. **Calculate Weighted Scores**

   Multiply the score by the weight of each criterion and sum up the total for each option.

Example: Family vs. Career

Let's create a prioritization matrix to decide between staying home for a family need or accepting a career advancement opportunity.

Criteria	Weight	Family Focus (Score)	Family Focus (Weighted)	Career Focus (Score)	Career Focus (Weighted)
Emotional Well-being	9	5	45	3	27
Financial Growth	7	2	14	5	35
Future Opportunities	8	3	24	5	40
Time Commitment	6	5	30	2	12
Total			**113**		**114**

Interpretation: The scores are very close, indicating a tough choice. However, the career focus slightly edges out due to its financial and future opportunity benefits. This framework also highlights that family concerns remain highly weighted, suggesting a blended or mitigated solution.

Pareto Analysis

The Pareto Principle (80/20 Rule) helps identify the critical few factors that contribute most to an outcome. When balancing family and career, this analysis can help pinpoint key drivers of satisfaction and success.

Steps to Use Pareto Analysis

1. **List Activities or Concerns**

   Identify all relevant activities or concerns for both family and career (e.g., kids' education, financial security, work-life balance).

2. **Assess Impact**

   Quantify the impact or importance of each activity in percentage terms. This could be based on time, emotional energy, or financial value.

3. **Cumulative Analysis**

   Rank activities by impact and calculate cumulative percentages.

   Example: Pareto Analysis for Family vs. Career

Scenario: You're weighing the decision to move for a job, balancing the impact on your family and career goals..

Activity/Concern	Impact (%)	Cumulative Impact (%)
Kids' Education	30	30
Spousal Job Adjustment	25	55
Financial Benefits	20	75
Proximity to Extended Family	15	90
Social Circle Adjustment	10	100

Interpretation: The top two concerns (kids' education and spousal job adjustment) account for 55% of the decision's weight. Addressing these first can simplify decision-making.

Combined Approach

By integrating both tools, you can create a more nuanced decision-making framework:

- Use the Pareto Analysis to identify the most critical factors
- Incorporate these factors into the Prioritization Matrix for a comprehensive evaluation

Example Table: Final Integrated Decision Framework

Criteria	Weight (Pareto)	Family (Score)	Family (Weighted)	Career (Score)	Career (Weighted)
Kids' Education	30	5	150	2	60
Spousal Job Adjustment	25	4	100	3	75
Financial Benefits	20	2	40	5	100
Emotional Well-being	15	5	75	3	45
Proximity to Family	10	5	50	2	20
Total	**100**		**415**		**300**

Decision: Family focus outweighs career focus (415 vs. 300), suggesting that family-related priorities are more critical in this scenario.

- **Structured Decisions:** Tools like Prioritization Matrix and Pareto Analysis transform emotional dilemmas into logical evaluations
- **Blend Data with Emotion:** These methods complement your instincts with data, ensuring balanced decisions
- **Dynamic Use:** Periodically revisit the framework as circumstances and priorities evolve

Dealing with New Entrants, Role Shifts, and Organizational Politics: Turning Disruption into Opportunity

Every workplace is like a living, breathing organism; constantly evolving, adapting, and shifting. With new faces entering the scene, job roles being redefined, and the ever-present dance of office dynamics, one thing is clear: change isn't optional, but how we respond to it is.

Sometimes, what looks like a threat is actually the start of a transformation. If we learn to reframe uncomfortable moments, we can turn confusion into clarity and tension into teamwork.

Growth rarely knocks politely; it often shows up as disruption in disguise.

Welcoming New People Without Feeling Replaced

When someone new joins, especially in a leadership or influential position, it can stir up feelings of being overlooked, underestimated, or even replaced. But here's the truth: every new entrant is also a new opportunity. Instead of pulling back, lean in.

Example:

In a global operations center, a seasoned employee initially felt threatened by an external hire. But instead of staying stuck in resentment, he chose a "Try Me" mindset; he initiated joint brainstorming sessions and offered to mentor the new colleague on internal systems.

The result? His role became more visible, his influence expanded, and he was later tapped for a special leadership project.

Lesson: Don't compete. Collaborate. When new energy enters the room, use it to recharge your own.

Role Shifts: Not an Exit, but a New Entrance

Job changes can feel like the rug is being pulled from under your feet, especially when you're not the one calling the shots. A lateral shift, a sudden promotion, or a new team assignment can shake your confidence.

But remember: discomfort is often the front door to growth.

Example:
A back-end support executive in an online travel firm was moved to a customer-facing role. Her initial reaction was, "I'm not good at this." But she turned it around: enrolled in a basic communication workshop, practiced daily interactions, and slowly built trust with clients.

Six months later, she received the "Customer Hero" award.

Lesson: Skill can be developed. Attitude can be chosen.

Making Peace with Organizational Politics

Workplace politics get a bad rap. But politics isn't just gossip or manipulation; it's about navigating influence, building trust, and aligning interests.

Ethical influence is a real skill, and when done right, it turns silos into synergies.

Example:
A department head noticed internal rivalries were slowing down project launches. Instead of choosing sides or staying silent, she initiated regular cross-functional huddles. She listened, understood root causes, and helped set shared OKRs. Her visibility and credibility grew; so, did her team's outcomes.

Lesson: Politics isn't the problem. Avoiding it blindly is.

How to Reframe Your Inner Dialogue: From Resistance to Resilience

The key to thriving in uncertain times lies in the stories we tell ourselves. Here's how to rewrite the script:

Practical Steps to Shift from "Why Me?" to "Try Me":

- Spot the Pattern:

  When doubt creeps in, pause, ask: Am I reacting from fear or stepping into possibility?

- Challenge Your Inner Narrator:

  Thoughts like "I'm not ready" or "They don't need me" often reflect insecurity, not truth. Replace them with "What if this is my stretch moment?"

- Speak Growth Language:

  Instead of "This isn't fair," try "What can I learn?" or "Where can I contribute most?"

- Network with the Right People:

  Surround yourself with peers, mentors, or leaders who support growth, not gossip.

- Start Small, Build Bold:

  Take one action each week outside your comfort zone. These small wins stack up fast.

Change doesn't ask for permission. It walks in, rearranges the furniture, and challenges your comfort. But every disruption carries a silent invitation: Will you resist it, or rise with it?

In a world of shifting roles and new dynamics, the most powerful position you can take is not authority; it's adaptability.

Key Challenges in Corporate Politics & Role Shifts

Challenge	Default Reaction (Escape Boat)	Reframed Mindset
New entrant in the team	"They're replacing me"	"They bring fresh perspective; I bring depth"
Missed promotion	"They overlooked me again"	"What feedback can I use to prepare better next time?"
Credit being stolen	"Why should I try at all?"	"How can I document my contributions and elevate my brand?"
Politics & favouritism	"I hate this toxic place"	"Where can I influence outcomes through value, not power games?"

Reframing the narrative from "Why me?" to "Try me" is a transformative step that empowers individuals to break free from The Escape Boat mindset. By embracing change, new entrants, and organizational politics as opportunities rather than threats, professionals can navigate their careers with resilience and purpose.

Opportunities don't always arrive wrapped as promotions or raises. Sometimes, they show up disguised as difficult people, unexpected competitors, or awkward transitions.

Your job is not to fight them.
Your job is to reframe them as your training ground.
Your moment to say, with full presence and power:
"Try me."

11 ABANDON THE ESCAPE BOAT:

WHY COLLABORATION SINKS COMPETITION

Collaboration Over Competition

We've all been on The Escape Boat, that mental life raft we jump onto when fear whispers:

"What if they outshine you? What if sharing credit means losing your worth?"

But here's the truth: The boat is leaking. Hoarding opportunities isolates us. True success? It's built on shared docks, not solo voyages.

Why This Matters: The World Isn't a Zero-Sum Game

From playgrounds to boardrooms, we're often conditioned to believe success is scarce, that for me to win, someone else must lose. It's a belief that fuels quiet rivalries, tension in teams, and toxic workplaces. But real progress, both personal and professional, doesn't come from tearing others down; it comes from lifting each other.

Collaboration is not just a "nice-to-have" skill anymore. It's the superpower that transforms workplaces, classrooms, families, and even communities.

Whether your age is 16, 36, or 66, the principle remains the same:
When we stop seeing each other as threats and start seeing each other as teammates, everyone wins.

What is Collaboration Over Competition?

It's a mindset. A belief that:

- Ideas grow better when shared
- Success isn't a limited resource

- There's more power in "we" than "me"

This doesn't mean giving up your ambition. It means redefining success as something collective, not just personal.

Imagine this:

- In school: Two students study together and both score higher
- In a corporate setup: Two departments share insights and double the customer impact
- At home: Siblings support each other, and the whole family feels more at peace

This is the power of shared wins.

From "Me" to "We": Creating Shared Wins

Why Collaboration Beats Competition

- **The Pie Expands**
    - o Myth: "There's only one slice of success"
    - o Reality: Collaboration bakes more pies

Example: Two rival chefs team up to open a pop-up. Their combined audience doubles sales.

- **Strength in Asymmetry**
    - o Your weakness is someone else's superpower

Example: A tech whiz (bad at sales) partners with a charismatic marketer. Result? A thriving app

- **Legacy > Ego**
    - o Competitors are forgotten. Collaborators become legends

Think: Jobs & Wozniak (Apple), Lennon & McCartney (The Beatles)

The Scarcity Trap

According to Harvard psychologist Dr. Carol Dweck (author of Mindset), individuals with a fixed mindset often fear others' success, which makes them feel small or behind. In contrast, those with a growth mindset see others' progress as a sign of what's possible for themselves, too.

> Collaboration activates the growth mindset.
>
> It says: "There's enough space for all of us."

From Threat to Team Player

At GreenSprout Agency, mid-level managers Sam and Pritha saw each other as threats.

- Both wanted the same promotion
- They hid ideas, fearing the other would "steal credit"
- Projects stalled. Morale plummeted

The Shift:

A mentor challenged them:

"What if you combined your strengths instead of guarding them?"

The Experiment:

- **Shared a Client Pitch**
    - o Sam's eye for design + Pritha data storytelling = A groundbreaking proposal

- **Co-Led a Workshop**
  - o Their contrasting styles (energetic vs. analytical) engaged all learners

- **Results:**
  - o Client landed ($200K deal)
  - o Both promoted (new roles were created)
  - o Culture shifted: Other teams copied their model

The Lesson:

When you drop the "us vs. them" mentality, you stop racing for scraps and start feasting at a bigger table.

Shared Wins in Action (Across Age Groups)

Age Group	Scenario	Collaboration Example
School Students	Group project	Dividing roles by strengths, one does research, and one presents
College Students	Startup pitch	Combining tech skills with design creativity for a standout presentation
Working Professionals	Cross-functional project	Marketing and IT teaming up to launch a successful digital campaign
Seniors & Communities	Volunteering efforts	Retirees organizing joint skill-sharing workshops with youth

Activity: The Collaboration Circle

Identify potential partners in your circle and unlock a shared win.

- Draw a circle. Write your name in the center
- Around it, write 5 people you regularly interact with
- For each, answer:
    - o What strengths do they have?
    - o What could we co-create?
    - o What's stopping us?
- Reach out to one person this week and start a small collaborative project, even if it's just a shared idea or discussion

The Tide Lifts All Boats

The Escape Boat's biggest lie? "You have to go alone to get ahead." But history's brightest breakthroughs? All crewed by teams.

'Throw out the paddles. Build a bridge instead.'

There's no scarcity of talent in the world, only a shortage of trust. The next time someone new enters your space, a colleague, a classmate, a teammate, don't tighten your grip.

Open your hands. Build something together. Because -

When we collaborate, we don't just win, we evolve.

12 STEER YOUR SHIP: SELF-LEADERSHIP TOOLS TO ESCAPE EXCUSES

Strategic Leaders: Born with Instinct or Built Through Insight?

Great leaders aren't simply born with a strategic mindset; they develop it through experience, reflection, and continuous learning. While some individuals may have a natural inclination toward big-picture thinking, strategic leadership is largely a learned skill. It involves analyzing trends, making informed decisions, and ensuring your actions match your long-term vision.

For instance, Satya Nadella, CEO of Microsoft, wasn't just handed a vision; he cultivated strategic insight by listening, learning from failures, and transforming company culture.

With the right mindset, mentorship, and exposure to real challenges, anyone can grow into a strategic leader.

Strategic thinkers aren't found; they're forged through intent, insight, and iteration.

Everyone knows that feeling; when fear quietly suggests, "Stay where it's safe." The Escape Boat tempts you to drift away from progress. But what if you could steer your course?

Self-leadership isn't about being fearless. It's about choosing courage over comfort, one small decision at a time.

"The toughest person you will ever lead... is yourself."

But there's good news: You have the power to retake control.

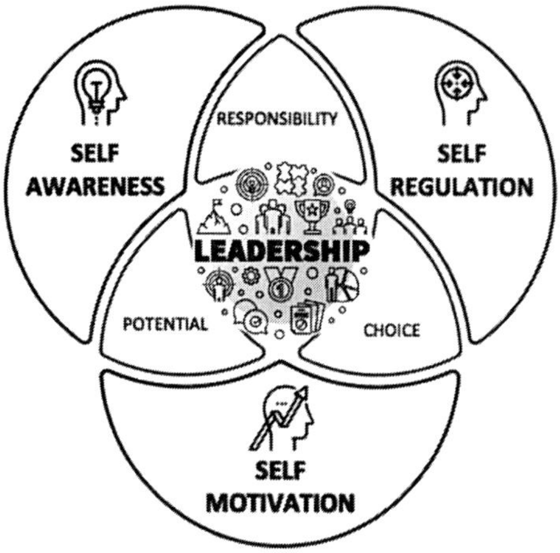

Self-leadership acts as your anchor when uncertainty threatens to sweep you away. It's what separates those who wait for change from those who become the change.

Let's dive into two powerful, practical tools that can help you build that muscle, one micro-action at a time.

The 5-Minute Courage Exercise

Because bravery isn't always loud; sometimes, it's just five minutes long!

When you feel the urge to escape (procrastinate, avoid, or make excuses), give yourself just 5 minutes to face it head-on.

This exercise is designed to activate your inner decision-maker, especially when you're tempted to escape or defer action.

Activity:

- Set a timer for 5 minutes

- Do the thing you're avoiding; whether it's sending that email, starting a project, or having a tough conversation
- After 5 minutes, decide: Keep going or pause? (Most people keep going; momentum is powerful!)

Why It Works:

- 5 minutes feels manageable (no overwhelming commitment)
- Action shrinks fear; once you start, the Escape Boat loses its power

Example:

- Avoiding the gym? Commit to 5 minutes on the treadmill. You'll likely stay longer
- Scared to pitch an idea? Speak up for just 5 minutes in the meeting. You'll gain confidence

According to Dr. Brené Brown (Daring Greatly), vulnerability and courage go hand in hand. Even tiny acts of courage can rewire your brain to trust yourself more and escape less.

Is It an Escape or a Strategic Pause?

Not every delay is bad; sometimes, waiting is wise. But how do you know if you're escaping or strategizing?

Here's your self-leadership checklist to audit your decision:

Question	Escape Boat Answer	Strategic Pause Answer
Why am I waiting?	"I'm scared to fail"	"I need more data to decide"
What's the cost of delay?	"I'll miss the opportunity"	"Rushing could hurt the outcome"
How will I feel after?	"Regretful for not acting"	"Confident I made the right call"

Example:

- Escape Mode: "I won't apply for the promotion yet; I'm not 'ready.'" (Fear)

- Strategic Mode: "I'll spend 2 weeks preparing a strong case, then apply." (Plan)

Self-leadership isn't about always knowing the way. It's about being willing to steer, even when it's hard.

'You don't have to roar to be brave. You just have to show up'

Activity:

Question	If Mostly "Yes" → It's an ESCAPE	If Mostly "Yes" → It's a STRATEGIC PAUSE
Am I avoiding discomfort?	Yes	No
Is fear driving this decision?	Yes	No
Am I waiting for the "perfect" moment?	Yes	No
Do I feel drained after deciding?	Yes	No
Do I have a clear reason and plan to revisit this?	No	Yes
Is this pause part of a bigger goal or strategy?	No	Yes
Will taking action right now cause harm or burnout?	No	Yes
Am I buying time to respond better, not avoid?	No	Yes

Save this checklist on your phone or desk. Whenever you feel yourself "floating," pause and quickly check in with yourself. Self-awareness is your anchor.

Whether you're a student hesitating to speak up in class, a mid-career professional unsure about a promotion, or a retiree questioning "what's next", The Escape Boat shows up for all of us.

However, self-leadership tools like these help us paddle toward growth, rather than drifting toward comfort.

So, the next time you feel yourself reaching for an excuse or waiting for the "right time", stop. Ask:

"Am I escaping, or am I growing?"
Then lead yourself; five minutes at a time.

SECTION IV –

FUTURE-READY IMPLEMENTATION & SUSTAINABILITY

13 THE AI-POWERED THE ESCAPE BOAT TOOLKIT

In today's rapidly changing digital world, staying innovative isn't a choice; it's essential for survival. Yet, even in tech-driven environments, professionals and organizations often board "The Escape Boat", avoiding bold decisions, delaying Digital Transformation, or resisting AI/ML adoption due to fear of complexity or failure.

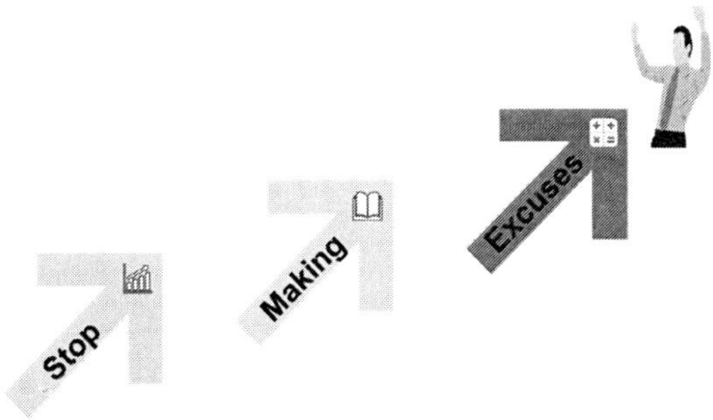

As technology continues to evolve at an unprecedented pace, future-ready organizations are embracing innovative methodologies, artificial intelligence, machine learning, and data science to drive implementation and sustainability. The Escape Boat Toolkit serves as a technological compass for navigating these complex waters, offering structured resources.

The key to sustainable innovation lies in structured execution. Below is a future-ready toolkit, powered by AI, behavioral science, and data-driven practices, to help you replace excuses with action at scale.

Building Strategic Thinking Capability: A Blend of Gift, Growth, and Grit

Strategic Thinking Capability (STC) isn't a universal formula; it's a unique blend of natural talent, learned experience, and regular practice. Endowment refers to natural talents, shaped by your genes and upbringing, like curiosity, pattern recognition, or problem-solving instincts.

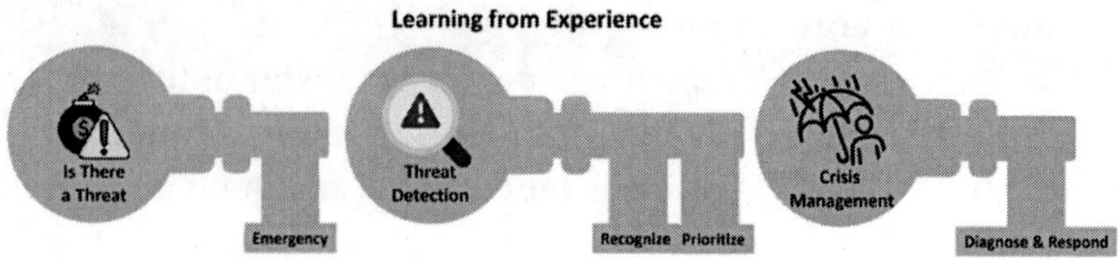

Experience adds the real-world lens; the knowledge you gain from roles, challenges, and decisions sharpens your judgment. Finally, exercise is all about conscious practice, asking better questions, mapping long-term impact, and making time to reflect.

Example:

A product manager may naturally spot trends early (endowment), learn from launching both failed and successful products (experience), and intentionally review market patterns every week (exercise); together, making them a sharp strategic thinker.

You can't control what you're born with, but what you do with it defines your strategic edge!

The Escape Boat Toolkit: Leveraging AI & Data for Smart, Sustainable Progress

In today's fast-paced world, moving forward isn't just about hard work; it's about working smart. This is where AI-powered self-audit tools and data-driven templates become game-changers. Whether you're in a corporate role, running a small business, leading a community initiative, or managing your household, these tools can help you move from "stuck" to "strategically in control."

Think of AI-powered self-audits as your compass. Instead of guessing what's working or not, AI tools like Tableau, Power BI, or even Excel with automation add-ins help you see real-time progress, spot issues before they grow, and make better choices. You're not reacting; you're leading with insight.

Templates backed by machine learning can take routine tasks off your plate. For example, Azure ML or TensorFlow can feed data into smart templates that update themselves based on past trends. If you're running a team project, this means your action plans evolve automatically as the situation changes. No more static planning; just dynamic, responsive strategy.

Use Case:

Imagine you're part of a marketing team aiming to segment customers for a new product. Instead of manually guessing who to target, an AI-driven worksheet using clustering algorithms (like K-Means) sorts customers based on behavior patterns. Now, your strategy is not only faster; it's smarter and more personalized.

"Smart tools don't replace your judgment; they elevate it."

Tools to Help You Stay Ahead in the Value Stream:

- Power BI/Tableau – for visual self-audits that reveal insights at a glance
- TensorFlow/Azure ML – for building predictive and adaptive templates
- AI-Enhanced Worksheets – for turning brainstorming into evidence-backed action

What Would It Take to Be There?

- Curiosity to Learn New Tools – not technical expertise, but a growth mindset is required

- Willingness to Experiment – use small pilots before scaling AI initiatives
- Collaboration Across Roles – involve people from tech, business, and operations to co-create smart, sustainable solutions

No matter your background or domain, the blend of Business rules, Body and Robots can guide you out of the "escape boat" mentality and into future-ready leadership. Let the tools work with you, not instead of you.

Case Study: Companies like Netflix use AI-driven self-audits to evaluate the efficacy of their recommendation algorithms, identifying gaps and refining user experience in real time.

Identify where you (or your team) default to avoidance patterns in innovation - (Run the below audit monthly via NLP-powered tools like Notion AI or ChatGPT Plugins) –

Escape Behavior	Tech Equivalent	AI Mitigation Strategy
"We're not ready for AI yet."	Resistance to automation adoption	AI Readiness Assessment (Tools: IBM Watsonx, Google's AI Adoption Framework)
"Our data isn't clean enough."	Analysis paralysis in Data Science	Automated Data Health Scan (Python + Great Expectations library)
"This innovation is too risky."	Fear of disruptive tech (e.g., GenAI)	Risk Simulation (Monte Carlo models in TensorFlow/ PyMC3)

- **Agile Implementation Worksheets**

Break innovation into sprints, not marathons.

Activity:
Worksheet: "30-Day Digital Transformation Sprint"
(Ideal for AI/ML, Cloud Migration, or Process Automation)

Week	Focus Area	AI/ML Tool to Test	Success Metric
Week 1	Data Readiness	Trifacta (Data Wrangling)	% of datasets pipeline-ready
Week 2	Proof of Concept (PoC)	Hugging Face Transformers	PoC accuracy vs. legacy system
Week 3	Stakeholder Buy-In	Power BI + GPT-4 Summaries	Leadership alignment score (1-10)
Week 4	Scalability Plan	AWS SageMaker Autopilot	Cost/ performance tradeoff analysis

We can use Jira AI or ClickUp Brain to auto-track progress.

- **Behavioral Reinforcement via AI**

Sustain change by predicting and preventing relapse into old habits.

Activity: AI Coach: "Escape Boat Alert System"

- Integrate with Slack/MS Teams via LangChain chatbots
- Detects hesitation keywords ("later," "not sure," "too early") in messages

- Sends personalized nudges:
    - o "You hesitated on the AI rollout; here's a 5-minute courage exercise."
    - o "Team discussion flagged 'risk aversion'; try a risk-scenario simulation."

Daily, Weekly, and Monthly Practices: Creating a Sustainable Ecosystem

Daily Practices:

- Data-Driven Decision Making: Using tools like AI-powered dashboards to review daily KPIs (Key Performance Indicator) and identify anomalies

- AI Automation: Automate routine tasks, such as email categorization or customer service query triaging, to save time and improve efficiency

Example: A company uses robotic process automation (RPA) for daily invoice processing, reducing errors and improving productivity

Weekly Practices:

- Feedback and Iteration: Set up weekly evaluations using machine learning insights to refine workflows and processes

- Collaborative AI: Use collaborative platforms like Microsoft Teams integrated with AI to promote innovation and brainstorming among team members

Example: A marketing team could analyze weekly social media trends using sentiment analysis to adjust campaigns dynamically.

Monthly Practices:

- Transformation Reviews: Conduct monthly strategic reviews using AI tools to assess long-term impacts and goals
- Learning Sessions: Organize deep-dive sessions with data science experts to explore innovations, from generative AI to explainable AI

Example: Organizations harness AI-based simulations to assess monthly financial health and predict risks in turbulent market conditions.

14 CREATING OPPORTUNITY RITUALS: FROM EVERYDAY MOMENTS TO LIFE-CHANGING MOVES

Rita, a school teacher from a small town, always dreamed of launching an educational YouTube channel. But between her day job, family, and self-doubt, she kept pushing the idea aside. One evening, she decided to dedicate just 15 minutes a day to jotting video topics in a diary. Within a month, she had over 20 ideas. Two months later, her first video went live. Now, she teaches thousands online; all because of a tiny, consistent ritual that transformed her hesitation into action.

Opportunities Don't Always Knock; Sometimes You Have to Build the Door

In life, the biggest chances don't come with flashing signs. Often, they arrive disguised as small decisions, routine moments, or even discomfort. That's why creating opportunity rituals; small, daily habits that help you stay alert and ready, is key to turning potential into progress. Without rituals, it's easy to drift into the comfort zone or hide in "The Escape Boat" of excuses. But with them, we shape our mindset to recognize, respond, and rise.

Making Action a Habit, Not a Hurdle

Habits are more than routines; they're systems that run our lives silently. If we design them well, they move us toward growth without needing willpower every day. Rituals don't have to be dramatic. Tiny actions, done repeatedly, build more momentum than occasional leaps.

Example:

A sales executive spends 10 minutes every morning scanning industry newsletters and sends one helpful insight to his team. Over time, he becomes a go-to thought leader and eventually, a team lead.

> "Big wins are born from small rituals. What you do daily becomes what defines you eventually."

How to Build Your Opportunity Rituals

1. Trigger-Based Action:

Associate a physical or digital cue with your new habit.

Example: Keep a sticky note on your laptop that reads: "What can I act on today?"

2. Reinforce with Rewards:

Celebrate small wins, even with something simple like crossing off a checklist or treating yourself to a coffee after completing a task.

3. Weekly Reflection Ritual:

Every Friday or Sunday, ask yourself:

- What opportunity did I say "yes" to this week?
- What did I avoid, and why?
- What can I tweak in my habit for next week?

4. Practice "Micro-Actions":

Break big dreams into 5-minute daily actions. Want to start a podcast?

Day 1: write name ideas.

Day 2: outline topics.

Day 3: test your mic.

Tiny steps still move you forward.

Tools to Keep You Aligned in the Opportunity Zone:

- Trello or Notion – for opportunity tracking and idea logging
- Habit trackers like Habitica or Streaks – gamify your rituals
- Time-blocking calendars (Google Calendar) – lock time for your "opportunity hour"

Whether you're a homemaker considering a new career, a college student unsure of the next move, or a seasoned professional thinking of reinvention, the answer lies not in waiting, but in creating. With consistent rituals, the gap between where you are and where you want to be gets smaller every day.

Your Opportunity Ritual Starts Now.
What's the smallest step you can take today?

Transforming The Escape Boat into an Action Plan

Excuses feel safe, but they keep us stuck. To transform "The Escape Boat" mindset into action, reframe your excuses as questions and goals.

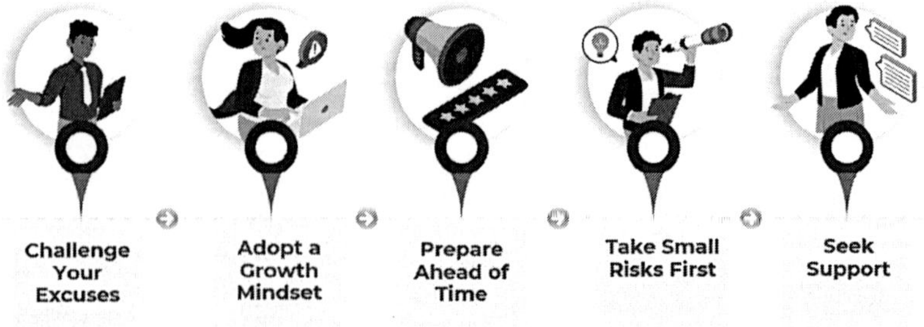

Here's how to shift the mindset:

- Challenge Your Excuses

"Is this a genuine reason or just fear talking?" This reflection can help differentiate between valid concerns and avoidance tactics

- Adopt a Growth Mindset

View opportunities as learning experiences, even if they come with risks. Success often stems from taking calculated chances

- Prepare Ahead of Time

Opportunities favor the prepared. Building skills, staying informed, and setting clear goals make decision-making easier

- Take Small Risks First

If big leaps feel daunting, start by taking smaller risks. This builds confidence and helps overcome fear of failure

- Seek Support

Mentors, friends, or colleagues can offer guidance and encouragement, helping you see opportunities more clearly

Behavior Change Models Simplified

While traditional models for behavior change can be complex, simplifying these concepts makes them accessible for real-world applications.

GROW Model: Unlocking a Growth Mindset & Breaking Free from Excuses

Excuses are the silent architects of stagnation. They disguise themselves as reason, caution, and logic, but in reality, they create invisible barriers that hold us back from opportunity and transformation. Whether you're a working professional, entrepreneur, student, or homemaker, learning to break free from excuses is essential for personal and professional growth. The GROW Model (Gain, Readiness, Openings, Willpower) offers a structured yet flexible approach to overcoming self-imposed limitations and embracing a growth mindset.

1. Gain: Strengthen Your Foundation

Growth starts with acquiring the right knowledge, skills, and insights to move forward. However, many people fall into the trap of believing, "I'm not ready yet" or "I don't have enough experience."

To eliminate this barrier:

- Shift from a fixed mindset (believing abilities are static) to a growth mindset (believing abilities improve with effort).
- Reframe excuses into empowering perspectives: instead of saying, "I don't know enough," ask, "What can I learn today to move forward?"
- Seek mentors, courses, and experiences that expand your abilities incrementally.

What is one small skill I can gain today to move closer to my goal?

2. Readiness: Prepare for Action

Readiness isn't about waiting for the "perfect time"; it's about creating the conditions that set you up for success. People often delay decisions, using phrases like "This isn't the right time" or "I don't feel prepared."

To eliminate this barrier:

- Recognize that progress beats perfection, start before you feel fully ready

- Build a support system that keeps you accountable and motivated
- Create a personal readiness ritual, such as setting daily intentions like "Today, I will say yes to one new opportunity"

What is one action I can take today to strengthen my readiness for future opportunities?

3. Openings: Identify & Seize Opportunities

Opportunities don't always arrive with flashing neon signs; sometimes, they require keen awareness and adaptability. Yet, many hesitate with questions like, "Would someone steal my thunder?" or "Do I have the right connections?"

To eliminate this barrier:

- Train yourself to spot and create opportunities, rather than wait for them to come to you
- Challenge limiting beliefs that convince you "Someone else is more qualified"; remember, initiative often outweighs experience
- Develop an opportunity journal to track ideas, openings, and missed chances, reinforcing a proactive mindset

What opportunity did I notice today that I would have overlooked before?

4. Willpower: Sustain the Drive to Move Forward

Momentum is fragile; without consistent effort and resilience, excuses creep back in. Many fall into patterns of avoidance, saying, "I tried, but it didn't work" or "Maybe it's not meant for me."

To eliminate this barrier:

- Strengthen your internal discipline by creating micro-habits that fuel consistency
- Reframe failures as feedback; instead of quitting, ask, "What adjustments can I make?"
- Celebrate small wins to maintain motivation and prevent burnout

What is one way I can fuel my willpower to keep moving forward?

Excuses have mastered the art of sounding reasonable, but they will never create progress. The GROW Model (Gain, Readiness, Openings, Willpower) helps dismantle barriers by offering actionable steps toward a growth mindset. Each step builds upon the other, moving individuals from hesitation to empowerment.

No more waiting. No more excuses. Growth begins the moment you decide to take the first step.

The Pattern Cycle: Breaking & Building Habits with Purpose

What is The Pattern Cycle?

The Pattern Cycle is the repetitive loop that governs our behaviors, both constructive and limiting. It consists of three key stages:

- Trigger
- Action
- Reinforcement

By understanding this cycle, individuals can identify unhealthy patterns and intentionally shape new, empowering habits.

Use Case: Overcoming Procrastination

Imagine a working professional who constantly delays important tasks due to distraction. Their Pattern Cycle looks like this:

- Trigger: Seeing an unread email, they feel overwhelmed and postpone responding
- Action: They open social media instead, seeking a temporary escape
- Reinforcement: The dopamine boost from scrolling makes this avoidance feel rewarding, reinforcing the habit

To reprogram the cycle, they must:

- Replace the Action; Commit to responding to one email immediately instead of escaping into distractions
- Reframe the Reinforcement; Celebrate small progress to make productive habits more rewarding

Activity: Rewriting Your Own Pattern Cycle

Try this simple exercise:

Category	Instruction	Response
Identify One Limiting Habit	(e.g., skipping exercise, avoiding tough conversations)	
Break Down the Cycle	What triggers it? How do you react? What reward reinforces it?	
Redesign the Cycle	Replace the reaction with an intentional action	
How will you reinforce it positively?		

Patterns Shape Futures

The Pattern Cycle dictates whether we evolve or remain stuck. By consciously interrupting negative loops and designing healthier cycles, anyone can rewire their behavior for success. The key? Consistency over perfection.

Understanding how behavior change works can make building new habits less intimidating.

Here are three simple, research-backed models:

1. Transtheoretical Model (Stages of Change):

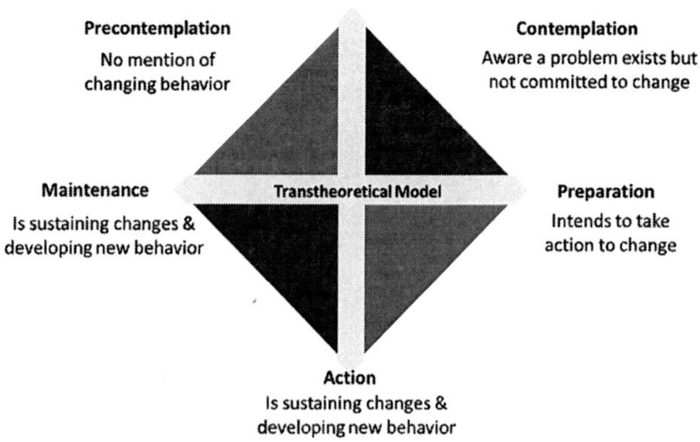

Change happens in stages:

- Precontemplation (not ready)
- Contemplation (thinking about it)
- Preparation (planning)
- Action (doing it)
- Maintenance (keeping it up)

Recognize your stage. If you're just thinking about transformation, focus on learning. If you're ready, set a small, specific action.

2. Social Cognitive Theory:

We learn by observing others and getting feedback. Surround yourself with people who take action and celebrate effort

Join groups or communities where opportunity-seizing is encouraged.

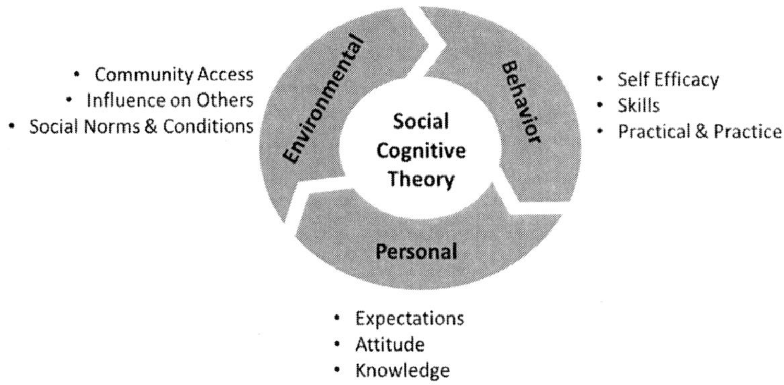

3. Small Step Strategy:

Begin with a small, intentional action, link it to a familiar routine, and acknowledge your progress immediately.

For instance, after enjoying your morning coffee, jot down one idea in your opportunity journal to cultivate a habit of proactive thinking.

Making Opportunity Rituals Sustainable

- Daily: Set a simple intention; "*Today, I will say yes to one new experience.*"

- Weekly: Reflect on the opportunities you encountered and the ones you embraced.
- Monthly: Assess your progress, refine your rituals, and establish a fresh "opportunity challenge" to keep momentum alive.

The emphasis is on consistent progress, not perfection. Each small action strengthens the foundation for larger breakthroughs.

Creating meaningful opportunity rituals involves embedding action into daily habits and applying simplified behavioral models to enhance adaptability and transformation. By understanding the dynamics of Capability, Possibility, and Determination, individuals can shape sustainable rituals that not only embrace possibilities but also foster long-term growth.

By distilling complex theories into actionable steps, anyone can transform fleeting moments into lasting success stories, one small step at a time.

15 THE MINDFUL MANAGER

Blending Spiritual Intelligence, Technology, and Management for a Future-Ready Corporate World and Leadership

As organizations become increasingly complex and dynamic, the role of a mindful manager takes on new significance. Incorporating spiritual intelligence, reflection, renewal, and resilience allows managers to not only drive performance but also nurture emotional, ethical, and technological growth within their teams. This integrated approach provides a framework for future-ready leadership that harmonizes technological advancements, spiritual values, and management principles.

The corporate world is evolving at breakneck speed; AI is reshaping workflows, remote teams span continents, and burnout is rampant. Amid this chaos, a new breed of leader is emerging: The Mindful Manager.

These leaders don't just chase KPIs; they cultivate Spiritual Intelligence (SQ), the ability to align purpose, empathy, and resilience in a high-tech world.

"Mindful Managers as the new world's people leaders"

Spiritual Intelligence in the Corporate World

Spiritual intelligence is the ability to apply spiritual principles, such as empathy, purpose, and interconnectedness, to navigate corporate environments effectively. Unlike conventional intelligence, which focuses on logic and analysis, spiritual intelligence emphasizes humanity, ethics, and deeper meaning in decision-making.

The Corporate Need for Spiritual Intelligence

In a rapidly transforming technological world, burnout, stress, and ethical dilemmas are common. A mindful manager equipped with spiritual intelligence can:

a. Foster Purpose-Driven Culture: Enable employees to connect their roles with the organization's mission, creating alignment and fulfilment

b. Promote Ethical Leadership: Encourage decision-making based on values rather than short-term gains

c. Strengthen Relationships: Build trust and cooperation across teams by valuing empathy and respect

Future-Ready Applications

Technological Synergy: Incorporate AI tools to analyze employee feedback and provide actionable insights for fostering meaningful workplace connections. Tools like sentiment analysis software can gauge emotional well-being and team cohesion.

Example: Leaders at Microsoft advocate a growth mindset culture, blending spiritual intelligence with technological innovation to create environments of trust and continuous learning

The Three R's of Mindful Leadership

A mindful manager integrates reflection, renewal, and resilience as cornerstones of leadership practice. These principles not only empower individuals but also create a framework for navigating change and challenges with clarity and strength.

A. Reflection: Pause and Analyze

Reflection involves taking time to evaluate past actions, challenges, and opportunities. In a corporate setting:

- Daily Practice: Set aside time for strategic reflection, such as reviewing outcomes of decisions and identifying lessons learned

- Technological Integration: Use data visualization tools like Tableau or Power BI for reflective analytics that provide insights into team performance or project success

Example: CEOs like Satya Nadella emphasize "learning from failures" through reflective practices that drive innovation and improvement.

B. Renewal: Energy Management in the Digital Age

Renewal emphasizes periodic rejuvenation to avoid burnout and sustain productivity.

- Spiritual Renewal: Encourage mindfulness or meditation practices for mental clarity

- Managerial Renewal: Advocate for skills development and engagement in creative endeavors to enhance leadership versatility

- Future-Ready Approach: AI-powered platforms like Headspace can be integrated into corporate wellness programs, offering guided meditation and stress management tools to employees

Example: A Salesforce executive credited her "5-5-5 Rule" (5 mins meditation, 5 mins nature, 5 mins no screens) for doubling her strategic output.

C. Resilience: Adapt and Thrive

Resilience is the ability to recover and grow through adversity. Managers can:

- Promote Agile Thinking: Foster adaptability through continuous learning and innovation

- Build Support Systems: Use collaborative AI tools to strengthen interpersonal connections, ensuring a safety net during tough times

Example: Companies like Google incorporate resilience training into employee programs, focusing on mental well-being and adaptive leadership.

The Future Belongs to Whole Leaders

The Mindful Manager thrives because they refuse The Escape Boat of burnout and soulless hustle. They merge:

- Technology (AI, data)
- Spirituality (purpose, presence)
- Management Science (agility, empathy)

The Mindful Manager represents the evolution of leadership, combining spiritual intelligence, technological foresight, and management wisdom to address the needs of tomorrow's corporate world.

By reflecting deeply, renewing actively, and building resilience, such managers serve as anchors in times of transformation. They embrace spiritual values alongside technological tools to create empathetic, innovative, and ethical workplaces.

In a future-ready organization, these principles are not merely aspirations; they are necessities. As we move into an era defined by change, the mindful manager stands at the crossroads of technology, spirituality, and leadership, guiding teams toward purpose, progress, and profound impact.

"The best leaders don't just manage time; they steward human energy in the age of machines."

SECTION V –

SUSTAIN & SCALE

16 FROM INDIVIDUAL TO ORGANIZATION: TURNING ESCAPE BOATS INTO OPPORTUNITY ENGINES

User Story: The Missed Turnaround

Rita, a mid-level HR manager in a retail firm, always felt her ideas weren't taken seriously. So, when her team was asked to redesign the employee engagement strategy, she quietly let others lead. A few weeks later, a colleague's idea, which was strikingly similar to hers, was applauded by leadership. Rita realized it wasn't the opportunity that was missing; it was her readiness to claim it.

This moment of hesitation, of letting "The Escape Boat" sail, reflects not just individual behavior but deeply rooted cultural patterns within organizations.

To sustain and scale successfully, whether at an individual or organizational level, one must move beyond momentary survival strategies to create systems that thrive and evolve. this transition requires understanding cultural symptoms of "escape boats", which represent reactive survival mechanisms, and fostering opportunity ecosystems in teams that enable growth and transformation. By addressing these elements, individuals and organizations can achieve lasting impact, ethical growth, and cultural resilience.

Cultural Symptoms of Escape Boats

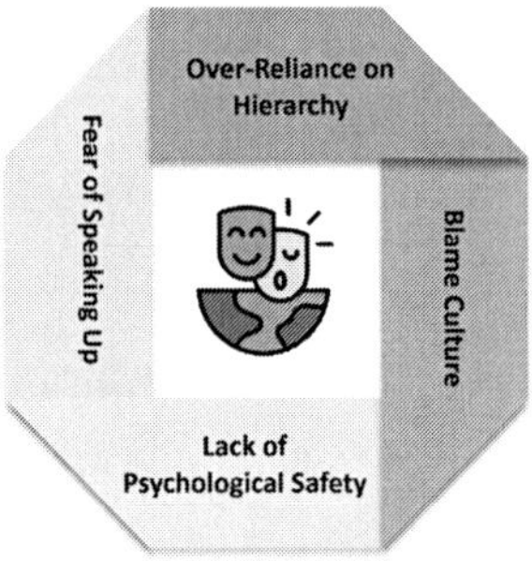

Escape boats represent a culture of reactive thinking, where people or teams focus solely on temporary solutions to avoid immediate challenges rather than addressing deeper systemic issues. These cultural symptoms can manifest in both individuals and organizations, leading to stagnation and missed opportunities.

Example: In a logistics firm, junior staff were reluctant to propose route optimization ideas. After creating a safe space to share, the company reduced delivery costs by 12% in just three months.

In any organization, whether a cutting-edge tech firm or a century-old manufacturing company, culture silently shapes behavior. When "The Escape Boat" mindsets begin to root themselves into a company's culture, they don't just affect individuals; they influence teams, departments, and eventually, the entire enterprise.

What are the Cultural & Common Symptoms of The Escape Boats?

- Short-Term Thinking: Prioritizing immediate results over sustainable strategies.

Example: A team under pressure rushes to deliver a project without considering long-term scalability, resulting in poor-quality outcomes that require frequent fixes later.

- Avoidance of Innovation: Teams shy away from suggesting bold ideas, fearing blame if things go wrong.

Example: In a corporate setting, team members might blame external factors rather than analyzing internal flaws that contributed to missed deadlines.

- Resistance to Change: Reluctance to embrace new ideas, leading to stagnation.

Example: An employee refuses to adopt advanced tools like AI-powered software, preferring outdated methods that slow progress.

- Over-Reliance on Hierarchy: People prefer escalating problems rather than owning them, using temporary solutions instead of addressing root causes.

Example: A company cuts costs by downsizing rather than optimizing workflows, only to face operational inefficiencies in the long run

- Blame Culture: When mistakes happen, the immediate reaction is to find a scapegoat instead of solutions.
- Toxic Comfort Zones: Mediocrity is tolerated because challenging the norm feels risky.
- Passive Compliance: Employees "follow the process" blindly without questioning outdated practices.
- Resistance to Change: Reluctance to embrace new ideas, leading to stagnation.

Example 1: Non-Technical

In a global insurance company, customer satisfaction scores were dipping, but no one raised it to leadership for months. Employees feared being seen as “negative.” Small problems snowballed, causing multimillion-dollar losses. Here, the cultural The Escape Boat wasn't incompetence; it was silence born out of fear.

Example 2: Technical

In a SaaS (Software-as-a-Service) firm, developers hesitated to migrate an old platform to a microservices architecture, even when they knew it was necessary. Why? "If we fail, the CTO (Chief Technical Officer) might lose trust in us." As a result, the tech debt grew until performance crashes forced an emergency migration under much worse circumstances.

Human Psychology Behind The Escape Boats

These cultural symptoms often stem from fear, insecurity, and a lack of trust within the organization. Individuals may resort to escape boats to avoid risk, criticism, or uncertainty. Addressing these symptoms requires fostering an environment of psychological safety, where failure is viewed as a learning opportunity rather than a setback.

Solution Framework

- Ethical Leadership: Leaders must demonstrate accountability, transparency, and empathy to instill trust
- Cultural Renewal: Introduce practices that promote reflection and continuous improvement
- Training Programs: Educate employees on long-term thinking and problem-solving techniques

Enabling Opportunity Ecosystems in Teams

An opportunity ecosystem is an environment where people are encouraged and equipped to spot, share, and act on ideas. This doesn't happen by chance. It's cultivated through structure, support, and shared success.

Opportunity ecosystems are environments designed to foster collaboration, innovation, and proactive growth. Unlike escape boats, opportunity ecosystems are intentional and strategic, enabling individuals and teams to identify, act on, and sustain opportunities.

Here's how to enable this transformation:

1. Make Opportunity a Habit

Integrate "opportunity check-ins" in team meetings.

Ask:

- "What's a small win we've ignored?" or
- "What can we try this week that we've never done before?"

2. Reward Effort, Not Just Results

Recognize employees who take initiative, even if the idea doesn't succeed. This promotes a growth mindset and shows that action matters more than perfection.

3. Open Doors for Cross-Pollination

Encourage employees to attend meetings outside their function or work on cross-team projects. Many breakthrough ideas come from seeing familiar problems with fresh eyes.

Key Principles

- Proactive Collaboration: Encourage teamwork that anticipates challenges and leverages diverse perspectives

Example: A product development team uses brainstorming sessions to envision future market needs and design scalable solutions.

- Skill Development: Invest in continuous learning to empower individuals to adapt and innovate

Example: Employees in a tech company undergo regular AI and data science workshops to stay ahead in their field.

- Supportive Culture: Create an environment of trust, respect, and shared purpose

Example: A manager acknowledges team members' contributions and provides mentorship, boosting morale and creativity.

"Opportunity isn't always a guest; sometimes, it's a mirror. Build a culture where people feel invited to see and act."

Tools That Help Teams Spot and Act on Opportunities

Technology's Role

Technology can amplify opportunity ecosystems by automating repetitive tasks, providing predictive analytics, and enabling seamless communication.

Platforms like Slack and Microsoft Teams, combined with AI-powered insights, can help teams collaborate effectively and identify growth areas.

Human Psychology in Opportunity Ecosystems

When individuals feel supported, valued, and inspired, they are more likely to embrace opportunities and take calculated risks.

Human behavior(s) thrives in environments that reward curiosity, encourage experimentation, and celebrate success.

Practical Steps to Create Ecosystems

- Mindful Management: Foster emotional intelligence and empathy in leadership practices.

- Shared Vision: Align individual goals with team and organizational objectives.
- Action-Oriented Rituals: Establish habits such as daily reflections, weekly team check-ins, and monthly strategy sessions to maintain momentum.

If organizations want to scale sustainably, they must shift from 'cultures of escape' to 'ecosystems of opportunity readiness'.

Here's how to nurture such an environment:

1. Promote Psychological Safety

Google's famous "Project Aristotle" (2016 research) found that psychological safety, the belief that one can take risks without fear of humiliation, was the #1 predictor of team success.

Action: Leaders must reward candor, thank team members for spotting risks early, and create platforms where every voice is heard, not just the loudest.

Use Case: A technology consulting firm launched monthly "Failure Fests" where teams shared projects that didn't meet targets, and what they learned. Over time, this boosted innovation by 27% as the fear of failure reduced.

2. Celebrate Micro-Risks

Micro-risks are small, calculated actions that challenge the status quo without large downside risks.

Action: Encourage team members to test new ideas on a small scale. Reward learning, not just winning.

Use Case: In a retail startup, a junior employee suggested automating customer returns using a chatbot. Instead of dismissing it, leadership greenlit a 2-week prototype. The bot saved 15% of customer service costs and inspired a wave of new tech initiatives.

3. Embed Ethical and Cultural Literacy

Technical knowledge alone is not enough. Every employee, from coder to cashier, should understand ethical decision-making and cultural awareness.

Action: Conduct workshops combining tech skills + ethical thinking. Teach employees how biases enter AI algorithms, how cultural differences impact user experience, or how unconscious bias affects hiring.

Inspire to Grow

Moving from escape boats to opportunity ecosystems is a transformative journey that requires cultural renewal, ethical leadership, and proactive habits. By understanding the psychological factors driving reactive behaviors and fostering supportive environments, individuals and organizations can sustain and scale effectively.

This approach inspires growth not just in skill or strategy but also in ethics, cultural awareness, and resilience. Whether you're a tech-savvy innovator or a non-technical visionary, embracing these principles can help you create a sustainable and thriving future, one opportunity at a time.

'The Escape Boat' Mindset teaches us that when fear drives decisions, both individuals and organizations shrink.

'The Opportunity Ecosystem' Mindset shows that when trust, learning, and ethics drive decisions, both individuals and organizations expand.

Whether you're a software engineer, an HR executive, a nurse, or a high school student, the message is simple:

Upgrade your knowledge constantly. Root yourself in strong ethical principles. Respect cultural diversity deeply. Become an opportunity creator, not just a survivor.

"The future will not reward just the smartest or fastest.
It will reward the boldly ethical and the culturally strong."

Activity: Signs Your Team is Falling into The Escape Boat Culture vs. Opportunity Culture"?

Checklist: Is Your Team Drifting in an Escape Boat or Rowing Toward Opportunity?

(Self-Assessment Template)

Aspect	Escape Boat Culture	Opportunity Ecosystem	Your Observation (Tick /Write Yes)
Risk-taking	Risk avoidance is common. People wait for approvals or play it safe.	Small experiments and micro-risks are encouraged and celebrated.	
Decision-making	Decisions are constantly delayed or escalated upwards.	Teams are empowered to make decisions within clear boundaries.	
Failure Handling	Failure is punished or hidden.	Failure is discussed openly and mined for learning.	
Innovation Mindset	Innovation ideas are seen as burdens or threats.	Innovation is part of everyday conversation and goal-setting.	

Aspect	Escape Boat Culture	Opportunity Ecosystem	Your Observation (Tick /Write Yes)
Psychological Safety	Speaking up is rare; silence is the norm.	Everyone feels safe to ask questions, challenge ideas, or admit mistakes.	
Ethical Courage	Ethical concerns are whispered, not raised openly.	Ethics and transparency are treated as leadership values, not barriers.	
Handling New People / Changes	New entrants are seen as threats to old roles.	New talents are welcomed as growth catalysts.	
Growth Focus	Comfort zones are protected fiercely.	Continuous learning is expected and supported.	
Feedback Culture	Feedback feels like criticism.	Feedback is framed as developmental and regular.	
Team Spirit	Competition overshadows collaboration.	Collaboration is seen as key to success.	

Instructions for Use:

- Review the list during team retrospectives or leadership offsites.
- Honestly, right tick / write Yes where your team fits today.
- Highlight 2-3 priority areas where small mindset or behavior shifts can create the biggest positive ripple.

Example Case: Mid-sized EdTech Company

After using the checklist, the leadership team realized they were operating mostly under an Escape Boat Culture in "Risk-taking" and "Failure Handling."

They initiated "Innovation Hours" every Friday afternoon, allowing employees to pitch new ideas without formal approvals, and started monthly "Lessons from Failures" sessions.

Within 6 months, employee engagement scores increased by 18%, and two new product lines emerged.

17 MENTORING THE NEXT ROWERS: PREPARING FOR FUTURE OPPORTUNITIES

How to Build Opportunity-Ready Teams

Opportunities are like currents in a river; they come unexpectedly, flowing with the potential to carry us forward or leave us behind. Mentoring the next rowers involves teaching readiness and building opportunity literacy within organizations. Leaders can foster a culture of growth and resilience by preparing individuals and teams to recognize, act upon, and sustain opportunities. This approach creates future-ready individuals and organizations, driven by ethical and adaptive strategies.

In a world where AI, automation, and rapid change are reshaping work, the most valuable skill we can teach isn't just technical expertise, it's

Opportunity Readiness: the ability to spot, seize, and shape opportunities before they slip away

But too often, organizations and individuals stay stuck on "The Escape Boat"; waiting for perfect conditions, fearing failure, or missing signals of change.

The solution? Mentorship that builds Opportunity Literacy, the fluency to recognize and act on possibilities.

What is Opportunity Readiness?

Opportunity Readiness is a mindset + skillset combo that helps people:

- Spot hidden chances (in challenges, trends, or gaps)
- Act before feeling "100% ready"
- Turn ideas into impact without over-analysis

Example:

- Low Opportunity Readiness: An employee sees a problem but thinks, "Not my job to fix it."

- High Opportunity Readiness: The same employee prototypes a solution and pitches it.

Teaching Opportunity Readiness: A Use Case

A mid-sized tech firm noticed junior employees were hesitant to propose ideas in meetings, waiting for "permission" or "more experience."

Solution: The "5-Minute Opportunity Drill"

1. Weekly Challenge: Mentors gave a real business problem (e.g., "How would you reduce customer onboarding time?").

2. 5-Minute Ideation: Juniors had to quickly brainstorm and share one actionable idea, no slides, just talking.

3. "Yes, and" Feedback: Leaders built on each idea (no shutting down).

Result in 3 Months:

- 43% more ideas flowed from junior staff
- 2 employee-led solutions were implemented (saving $150K/year)
- Culture shifted from "Wait for instructions" to "Try and iterate"

Prescribed Tool: Miro or Mentimeter for real-time collaborative ideation

Building an Opportunity-First Culture: From Escape to Embrace

In every organization, there's an invisible boat, "The Escape Boat." It's the one people climb into when they fear change, worry about failing, or feel it's safer not to try. But real growth happens when we stop rowing away from risk and start sailing toward opportunity.

Here's how individuals and organizations can build Opportunity Literacy: the skills, mindset, and rituals that help us spot, shape, and seize opportunities every day.

1. Reframing Risk: From Fear to Fuel

Escape Boat Thinking: "What if we fail?"

Opportunity Mindset: "What can we learn from this?"

In high-performing teams, the word "failure" is not a red flag; it's a signpost for growth. Instead of punishing mistakes, celebrate smart failures, the ones made in pursuit of innovation or customer delight.

Example: A mid-sized consulting firm added a "Learning Spotlight" in their internal newsletter. Every month, they shared a project that didn't go as planned, along with the lessons learned and what they'd do differently next time. The result? A culture where employees dared to try bold ideas without fear.

"What if failure was just fast learning in disguise?"

2. Ritualizing Opportunity Spotting

Opportunity isn't a lucky accident; it's a skill that can be trained. Just like brushing your teeth or having your morning coffee, make spotting opportunity a habit.

Activity: Host monthly "Horizon Scanning" sessions where teams answer:

- "What new trends are shaping our space?"
- "What customer complaints hint at unmet needs?"
- "What ideas are quietly working elsewhere?"

Tools: Use platforms like Exploding Topics, Google Trends, or ChatGPT to kick-start insights.

Example: A retail chain used trend analysis and AI chat prompts to identify a rising demand for sustainable packaging before it became mainstream, giving them a head start on redesigning their product line.

"What we see depends on what we look for. Are you looking for threats or opportunities?"

3. Redefining Mentorship: From Answers to Autonomy

Today's workplace needs mentors who guide, not prescribe; coaches who ignite curiosity, not control.

Instead of saying: "Here's exactly how to do it."

Activity: "Here's the challenge: what would you try first?"

Use case: Atlassian's "ShipIt Days" give employees 24 hours to solve any problem creatively, without managerial hand-holding. Some of their best tools and features have emerged from these free-thinking marathons.

Future-Proofing Mentorship Across Generations

Mentorship should evolve with the times. One size doesn't fit all, here's how to make it stick:

For Gen Z & Millennials:

- Encourage micro-challenges like: "Spot and fix one inefficiency this week."
- Let them pitch ideas in formats they love, like short videos or reels.

For Mid-Career Professionals:

- Try reverse mentoring: pair them with juniors to learn about Gen Z trends, AI tools, or social shifts.

For Leaders:

- Model "Unlearning": Share openly about how you adapted. Maybe you resisted AI initially, but embraced it once you saw the results. Vulnerability builds trust and inspires others to evolve.

"When leaders show they're learning, it gives others permission to try."

Your Turn: Make Opportunity Literacy Real

Today: Ask a teammate, "What's one idea we've been ignoring?"

This Week: Run a 5-minute Opportunity Drill, pose a problem and let your team brainstorm fast ideas.

This Month: Add "Opportunity Spotting" as a recurring item in your team meetings.

The Escape Boat feels safe, but it never reaches new shores. The ocean of opportunity may seem uncertain, but it's where the future lives. So… who will you invite to row with you?

18 THE FEEDBACK LOOP: YOUR GPS FOR GROWTH

Imagine driving a car with no GPS (Global Positioning System), no road signs, and no mirrors. You might move forward, but you'd have no idea if you're headed in the right direction or about to hit a dead end.

That's what life feels like without a Feedback Loop.

Whether you're a student, a CEO, an artist, or a parent, feedback is the mirror that shows you the blind spots you can't see on your own. But here's the catch: Most people avoid it, fear it, or ignore it, because it's uncomfortable.

Yet, the ones who actively seek and use feedback? They're the ones who grow faster, adapt smarter, and navigate life with clarity.

Why Feedback Loops Matter

1. Continuous Self-Awareness: The Key to Unlocking Potential

Self-awareness isn't a one-time thing. It's like a muscle; you have to keep exercising it.

Example: A study at Columbia University found that professionals who solicited feedback at least once a month were rated 32% more competent by their peers than those who didn't. (Reference: "Insight" by Tasha Eurich)

Use Case:

Without Feedback: A talented graphic designer keeps creating work she loves, but clients keep rejecting it. She assumes they "don't get her vision."

With Feedback: She asks one client, "What's missing?" They say, "Your designs are beautiful, but don't align with our brand voice." Now she adapts and wins more projects.

"You can't fix what you don't see. Feedback is the flashlight in the dark."

2. Creating a Personal Navigation System

A Feedback Loop works like a GPS for your growth:

- Input (Asking for Feedback): "How did I do?"
- Processing (Reflecting): "What does this mean?"
- Output (Adjusting): "What will I do differently?"

Example for Different Life Phases:

Students: A high-schooler asks his teacher, "Where did I lose marks in this essay?" He learns his arguments lacked evidence, next time, he researches better and scores higher.

Professionals: A salesperson reviews lost deals with her manager. She discovers she talks too much instead of listening. She practices active listening and closes 20% more sales.

Parents: A dad asks his teen, "Do I interrupt you too much?" The teen says yes. Dad works on pausing; their relationship improves.

Activity:

"The 5-Minute Feedback Sprint"

After any task (presentation, project, conversation), ask one person:

"What's one thing I did well and one thing I could tweak?" Write it down. Act on it within 24 hours.

The 3 Biggest Feedback Myths (And How to Break Them)

Myth 1: "Feedback means I did something wrong."

Reality: Feedback isn't blame; it's just information to help you do better.

Think of feedback like an app update. It's not saying the current version is broken; it's just offering an upgrade to work more smoothly.

Myth 2: "I know myself well enough; I don't need feedback."

Reality: Most of us see only parts of ourselves. Studies show that very few people are truly self-aware.

Ask three people you trust this:

"What's one thing I do well that I might not notice, and one area where I could improve?"

You'll be surprised at what you learn.

Myth 3: "Negative feedback will crush my confidence."

Reality: Ignoring feedback holds you back more than hearing something tough ever will.

If someone gives you honest feedback, say:

"Thank you; I value your perspective."

Even if it's hard to hear, it's often what helps you grow the most.

How to Build Your Feedback Loop (Step-by-Step)

1. Seek It Proactively

- At Work: After meetings, ask, "What could I have done better?"
- In Relationships: "Did I listen well, or did I interrupt?"
- For Creators: Post a draft and ask, "What's confusing or missing?"

2. Filter It Wisely

Not all feedback is equal. Ask:

- Is this person qualified to give it?
- Is it specific and actionable?
- Does it align with my goals?

3. Act on It Immediately

Small tweaks > Big overhauls
Example: A writer gets feedback that her intro is too long. Next piece, she cuts it by 30%; readers engage more.

Your Turn: Start Your Loop Today

Pick one area to improve (e.g., communication, productivity, parenting).

- Ask for feedback from someone today.
- Adjust one small thing based on what you hear.

"Feedback is the breakfast of champions. Are you hungry enough to grow?"

Beyond the Escape: Real Growth Begins When You Row

The Story We All Live In

Imagine you're standing on the shore of a peaceful lake. Behind you is your comfort zone: calm, familiar, and easy. Ahead lies a new land, full of possibilities, challenges, and growth. Floating in between? A small boat. It's not dangerous, but it keeps you in one place. This boat is full of excuses, fears, and reasons to wait. We all have one. It's called The Escape Boat.

But here's a truth that life proves over and over again:

> "You weren't built to float. You were built to row."

What Happens When You Choose to Row

Rowing isn't just movement.
It's an action
It's energy
It's progress

Every stroke makes you stronger. Every wave you push through builds resilience. You don't just reach new shores; you become a new version of yourself.

Real People | Real Choices | Real Growth

1. A Student Faces Setback, Not Surrender

Story: Priya, a first-year medical student, fails her anatomy exam. The boat whispers, "This isn't for you."

Rowing Moment: Instead of quitting, she joins a study group, starts daily revision, and asks for help.

Outcome: She passes with flying colors and learns perseverance, not just medicine.

2. A Manager Learns to Lead with Courage

Story: Raj avoids giving honest feedback to a struggling teammate. “Maybe it’ll sort itself out,” says the boat.

Rowing Moment: He takes a breath, speaks with empathy, and initiates a meaningful conversation.

Outcome: The teammate improves, and Raj earns respect as a trusted leader.

3. An Artist Turns Rejection into Recognition

Story: Meena’s novel gets rejected by 20 publishers. The boat tells her, “You’re not meant for this.”

Rowing Moment: She self-publishes, promotes her work online, and grows a loyal readership.

Outcome: Her third book is picked up by a major publishing house.

"The Escape Boat keeps you safe.
Rowing takes you somewhere new."

Rethinking What Success Looks Like

Society often defines success by job titles, bank balances, or how many likes you get online. But those are outcomes. True success starts with two things:

1. Self-Awareness: The Mirror That Matters

People stuck in the boat often say,
“My boss doesn’t understand,” or
“It’s not the right time.”
But those who grow ask, “What can I do differently?”

Activity:

Keep a "What I Learned" journal each week:

- One win you're proud of
- One mistake and what it taught you

Inspired by: The Daily Stoic by Ryan Holiday – A tool for daily reflection and personal growth.

2. Action: Starting Before You're Ready

People in The Escape Boat wait for the perfect moment. Those who row start before they feel ready.

Examples:

- Want to get healthy? Start with one walk today, not on Monday.
- Considering a career switch? Send one message to someone in your dream field this week.

Science says: Taking small steps reduces anxiety and builds momentum. (as per Harvard Business Review, "The Power of Small Wins")

"Confidence comes after action, not before."

How to Step Out of the Boat (For Good)

1. Know Your Escape Triggers

Ask yourself: When do I avoid action?

- Is it before tough conversations?
- When things feel uncertain?
- When you fear judgment?

Awareness is the first step to change.

2. Redefine What Failure Means

Escape Boat Mindset: "I failed, so I must not be good enough."
Rowing Mindset: "I failed, so now I know what not to do."

Example: Sir James Dyson created 5,126 failed vacuum prototypes before getting it right.

His motto? "Fail forward."

3. Build a "Rowing Ritual"

Make growth a daily habit.

- Daily: Do one thing that stretches you
- Weekly: Reflect on what you avoided, and why
- Monthly: Celebrate the courage, not just results

Your Turn: Grab the Oar

- Today: Name one "The Escape Boat" in your life, a fear, a delay, or a story you've been telling yourself
- This Week: Take a small rowing step against it
- This Month: Look back and ask: "How has rowing changed my direction?"

"The Escape Boat feels safe… but it quietly steals your future. The real journey begins when you pick up the oar and row toward growth, not away from fear."

CONCLUSION: BEYOND THE BOAT

The Journey of Growth and True Success

Life is not about waiting for the perfect wave; it's about rowing, even when the waters are rough. Every stroke you take builds strength, resilience, and progress. When you row, you grow. And as you move forward, you begin to see success differently, not just as an end goal, but as the awareness of your journey and the courage to keep going.

When You Row, You Grow

Imagine sitting in a boat, drifting with the current. If you do nothing, the river will take you wherever it flows, maybe to calm waters, maybe to a rocky shore. But when you pick up the oars and row, you take control.

- Rowing builds muscle. Every challenge you push through makes you stronger
- Rowing teaches patience. Progress isn't instant, it's a series of consistent efforts
- Rowing reveals direction. Action clarifies purpose; movement eliminates doubt

Growth doesn't happen in comfort. It happens when you push past hesitation, when you embrace effort over ease. The more you row, the farther you go, not just in distance, but in wisdom, confidence, and capability.

Redefining Success Through Awareness and Action

Society often defines success in terms of wealth, fame, or power. But true success is deeper; it's about awareness (knowing what truly matters) and action (living in alignment with it).

1. Success as Awareness

- Recognizing that happiness isn't just at the destination but in the journey
- Understanding that failure isn't the opposite of success; it's part of it
- Realizing that comparison steals joy; your path is yours alone

2. Success as Action

- Choosing courage over comfort
- Showing up even when motivation fades
- Measuring progress by effort, not just outcomes

When you combine awareness with action, success stops being a distant trophy and becomes a daily practice. It's in the small wins; the decision to try, the resilience to continue, the wisdom to adapt.

The Choice Is Yours: Row or Drift?

You will always have two choices:

- Drift – Let life happen to you, react to circumstances, and wonder why things never change

- Row – Take ownership, embrace challenges, and shape your destiny

The oars are in your hands. The boat moves when you do.

So, what will you choose?

"Growth Comes from Action, And True Success Is a Mindset, Not Just an Achievement!"

REFERENCE

Books (Behavioral, Psychological, Corporate Strategy, Spirituality)

Psychology & Human Behavior

- Kahneman, D. (2011). Thinking, Fast and Slow. New York: Farrar, Straus and Giroux.

- Tolle, E. (2004). The Power of Now: A Guide to Spiritual Enlightenment. Novato, CA: New World Library.

- Clear, J. (2018). Atomic Habits: An Easy & Proven Way to Build Good Habits & Break Bad Ones. New York: Avery.

- Pink, D. H. (2009). Drive: The Surprising Truth About What Motivates Us. New York: Riverhead Books.

- Pressfield, S. (2002). The War of Art: Break Through the Blocks and Win Your Inner Creative Battles. New York: Black Irish Entertainment.

- Brown, B. (2010). The Gifts of Imperfection. Center City, MN: Hazelden.

- Dweck, C. S. (2006). Mindset: The New Psychology of Success. New York: Random House.

Corporate & Leadership

- Sinek, S. (2014). Leaders Eat Last: Why Some Teams Pull Together and Others Don't. New York: Portfolio.

- Lencioni, P. (2002). The Five Dysfunctions of a Team: A Leadership Fable. San Francisco: Jossey-Bass.

- Bridges, W. (2009). Managing Transitions: Making the Most of Change (3rd ed.). Philadelphia: Da Capo Lifelong Books.

Spiritual & Philosophical Insight

- Frankl, V. E. (2006). Man's Search for Meaning. Boston: Beacon Press.
- Singer, M. A. (2007). The Untethered Soul: The Journey Beyond Yourself. Oakland, CA: New Harbinger Publications.
- Easwaran, E. (2007). The Bhagavad Gita (Classics of Indian Spirituality). Tomales, CA: Nilgiri Press.

Emotional Intelligence & Therapy

- Goleman, D. (1995). Emotional Intelligence: Why It Can Matter More Than IQ. New York: Bantam Books.
- Harris, R. (2008). The Happiness Trap. Boston: Trumpeter.
- David, S. (2016). Emotional Agility: Get Unstuck, Embrace Change, and Thrive in Work and Life. New York: Avery.
- Harris, R. (2011). The Confidence Gap. Boston: Trumpeter.
- Beck, J. S. (2011). Cognitive Behavior Therapy: Basics and Beyond (2nd ed.). New York: Guilford Press.

Habits, Purpose & Workplace Culture

- Duhigg, C. (2012). The Power of Habit: Why We Do What We Do in Life and Business. New York: Random House.

- Fogg, B. J. (2019). Tiny Habits: The Small Changes That Change Everything. New York: Houghton Mifflin Harcourt.
- Seligman, M. E. P. (2011). Flourish: A Visionary New Understanding of Happiness and Well-Being. New York: Free Press.
- Grant, A. (2013). Give and Take: Why Helping Others Drives Our Success. New York: Viking.
- Keswin, E. (2019). Bring Your Human to Work. New York: McGraw-Hill Education.
- Covey, S. R. (1989). The 7 Habits of Highly Effective People. New York: Free Press.
- Schein, E. H. (2010). Organizational Culture and Leadership (4th ed.). San Francisco: Jossey-Bass.
- Edmondson, A. (2019). The Fearless Organization: Creating Psychological Safety in the Workplace for Learning, Innovation, and Growth. Hoboken, NJ: Wiley.
- Edmondson, A. (2023). The Right Kind of Wrong: The Science of Failing Well. Atria Books.
- O'Neill, K. (2018). Tech Humanist: How You Can Make Technology Better for Business and Better for Humans. New York: Wiley.

Key Academic Articles and Whitepapers

- O'Keefe, P. A., Horberg, E. J., Lee, F., & Dweck, C. S. (2022). Implicit Theories of Opportunity. Journal of Personality and Social Psychology.

- Steel, P. (2007). Procrastination, Self-Regulation Failure, and Opportunity Costs. Psychological Bulletin, 133(1), 65–94.
- Umphress, E. E., Bingham, J. B., & Mitchell, M. S. (2010). Unethical Behavior in the Name of the Company. Journal of Applied Psychology, 95(4), 769–780.
- Edmondson, A. (1999). Psychological Safety and Learning Behavior in Work Teams. Administrative Science Quarterly, 44(2), 350–383.
- Hobfoll, S. E. (1989). Conservation of Resources: A New Attempt at Conceptualizing Stress. American Psychologist, 44(3), 513–524.
- Alemdar, M., & Anılan, H. (2020). Emotional Literacy Skills Scale: Development and Validation. International Journal of Contemporary Educational Research.

Business Insights, Reports & Magazine References

Harvard Business Review

- "Why We Hesitate to Seize Great Opportunities"
- "Leading in Uncertain Times: Cognitive Biases that Hold Back Managers"
- "Creating a Culture of Courage"
- "Collaborative Overload" (2016)
- "Why Smart Failure is a Good Thing" (2017)

McKinsey & Company

- "The Psychological Safety Imperative"
- "Why Middle Managers Are Stuck and What to Do About It"
- "Rewiring Organizations for the Age of AI" (2023)

Deloitte Insights

- "The Mind of the Manager in Crisis"
- "Opportunity Readiness Index"

Ethics & Compliance Initiative

- (2021). Global Business Ethics Survey. ethics.org

Supporting Tools & Frameworks

- GROW Coaching Model – Goal, Reality, Options, Will.
- SCARF Model – David Rock (NeuroLeadership Institute).
- Ikigai Framework – Japanese concept for purpose alignment.
- COM-B Model – Behavior change framework (Michie et al., 2011).
- Atlassian Team Playbook – ShipIt Days & Innovation Culture.

Case Studies & Corporate Failures

- Healy, P. M., & Palepu, K. G. (2003). The Fall of Enron. Journal of Economic Perspectives, 17(2), 3–26.

- Tiwari, R. P. (2010). Satyam Scandal: A Corporate Governance Failure. Indian Journal of Corporate Governance.

- The Verge. (2024, October 10). Marriott agrees to pay $52 million fine over data breach. The Verge.

Digital & ResearchGate Resources

- Meller, W. (2022). The Psychology of Saying No at Work. [https://williammeller.com]

- Frontiers in Psychology. (2021). Moral Emotion and Unethical Behavior.

- ShineSheets. (2025). Emotional Literacy: A Vital Skill for Everyone.

- CollegeNP. (2025). Emotional Intelligence: Essential for Success.

- Mullins Coaching. (2023). Competition to Collaboration.

- Tagvault.org – Excuses vs. Reasons.

- LynnLokPayne.com – Seizing New Opportunities.

- Peerdh.com – Transform Excuses into Actionable Goals.

- Times of India – Habit Formation and Psychological Insights.

- EUFIC & JMIR – Behavior Change Strategies.

- ResearchGate – Various articles on cybersecurity behavior, team dynamics, stress, and leadership.

Online Learning & Knowledge Portals

- The Open University. OpenLearn. https://www.open.edu/openlearncreate/
- Criterion HCM. Blogs on unethical behavior. https://www.criterionhcm.com/
- Zoho Workplace Articles. https://www.zoho.com/workplace/
- Psychologs. https://www.psychologs.com/
- Exploding Topics. (2024). AI-driven trend forecasting. https://explodingtopics.com/
- LinkedIn Articles.
  - Ela Mylek on hesitation and decision-making.
  - Anilesh Mukherjee on "Career! Do you know what you want"

Glossary: The Escape Boat

Anchor Statement

A short, powerful line you repeat daily to ground yourself emotionally and mentally, like a personal mantra that keeps you steady during challenging times.

Bias Toward Action

The habit of doing something rather than overthinking it. It's the mindset of "start small, but start now."

Comfort Zone

A mental space where everything feels safe, familiar, and easy, but staying here too long often leads to stagnation, not growth.

Emotional Literacy

The skill of recognizing, understanding, and naming your feelings, and using that insight to make better decisions and build deeper connections.

The Escape Boat

A metaphor for the excuses, justifications, or thought patterns we use to avoid growth, difficult conversations, or new opportunities.

Escape Pattern Detector

A self-awareness tool to help identify whether you're making a smart decision or just running away from discomfort, fear, or uncertainty.

Excuse vs. Reason

An excuse keeps you stuck and avoids responsibility. A reason acknowledges limitations honestly and looks for growth anyway.

Feedback Loop

A personal growth cycle where you actively seek input, reflect on it, apply changes, and repeat to improve consistently.

Impostor Syndrome

The internal feeling of being a fraud, even when you're qualified and capable. It often sounds like "I don't deserve this role" or "I just got lucky."

Learned Helplessness

A mindset developed over time when you feel that nothing you do makes a difference, leading to passive behavior and low self-belief.

Micro-Risks

Small, low-stakes actions taken outside your comfort zone that build confidence and prepare you for bigger decisions later.

Mindset Blocks

Internal beliefs or fears, like "I'm not good enough" or "I don't belong here", that keep you from acting, even when opportunity is present.

Opportunity Literacy

The ability to recognize, prepare for, and act on life or career opportunities in a mindful and strategic way.

Opportunity Window

A short period where change is possible, but only if you're aware, prepared, and courageous enough to act.

Opportunity Ritual

A set of intentional habits or routines designed to help you stay alert, focused, and ready to embrace growth moments.

Reframing

Changing how you look at a challenge, so it turns from a threat into a chance to grow.

Scarcity Mindset

A belief that there's not enough success, love, or recognition to go around, so if someone else wins, it means you lose.

Self-Leadership

Leading your own life with intention, values, and responsibility, especially when no one else is guiding you.

Strategic Pause

A conscious break to reflect, reset, and realign; not an escape, but a chance to return stronger.

Toxic Comparison

Measuring your worth against others in a way that drains motivation and damages self-esteem.

Value Stream

The set of activities or roles where you add the most meaningful, visible impact to your organization or life.

Whirlpool Effect

The mental or workplace cycle where you feel stuck, overwhelmed, or lost, despite being busy. Often fueled by unclear goals, burnout, or misalignment.

"Try Me" Mindset

A proactive attitude that welcomes challenge and growth instead of avoiding it. It says, "I might not be perfect, but I'm willing to try."

ABOUT THE AUTHOR

Om Sharma

Om is a benchmarking multi-industry expert with more than

two decades of experience in driving business excellence, people-first management, and digital transformation across Banking & Finance, Healthcare, Travel, and Telecom in BPO, KPO, IT, ITeS, GCC space. A Certified Master Black Belt in Lean Six Sigma, a customer experience operating centre (COPC) implementation expert, and has strengthened his management skills through the Harvard Business Publishing Management Series Program.

A renowned speaker in the field of customer experience and business excellence in different forums across Asia. He has also helped firms in Europe, Australia and the USA in building a culture of process re-engineering and transforming through automation and business process management to build efficiencies. A promoter of adding value to the book of knowledge (BoK) in literature for research. He holds a few international journal publications in the field of in the field of TQM, Emerging Technologies for Innovation, and Service Quality like IJARSM, IJSR, and ANQ Tokyo (Academia.edu).

He has been awarded with his work with few accolades, like "50 Most Talented Quality Professionals of India" by the Asian Confederation of Business", "Six Sigma Champion", "Six Sigma Professional of the Year award" awards by Golden Star Six Sigma awards and "Quality Leader of the Year" by World Quality Congress & Awards.

Learning never stops, he is a PhD scholar in the field of Information Systems and Operations, concentrating on levers of firm performance through the usage of emerging technologies and keeping the basics on for process re-engineering, and then Automate and Transform at Alliance University, India.

Anilesh Mukherjee

Anilesh is a transformation strategist and people-centric leader with over 17 years of experience driving Digital innovation, Operational Excellence, and AI-led enterprise growth across ITES, Healthcare, Education, Manufacturing and Startup Ecosystems. A certified Six Sigma Master Black Belt from the Indian Statistical Institute, a postgraduate from IMT Ghaziabad, and has deepened his strategic expertise through Harvard's Sustainable Strategy program.

Known for combining deep technical knowledge with empathetic leadership, Anilesh has successfully led large-scale transformations, modernising processes, building high-performing teams, and aligning technology with human behaviour to enable sustainable change. His consulting expertise has empowered startups and global enterprises alike to scale operations, navigate disruption, and foster innovation.

A published thought leader, Anilesh has authored widely acclaimed research papers and articles on AI, Lean Six Sigma, NLP, and intelligent automation. His previous book, "Sacred Synergy at MahaKumbh: Uniting Spirituality, Science, and Technology," received an overwhelming response for its unique blend of strategic insight and cultural depth.

At the intersection of data, leadership, and purpose, Anilesh continues to inspire organisations to lead with agility, emotional intelligence, and forward-thinking transformation.

Feel free to contact us at mukherjeeanilesh@gmail.com